Emily Post's

Favorite Party
& Dining Tips

Emily Post's

Favorite Party & Dining Tips

Peggy Post

Collins

An Imprint of HarperCollins*Publishers*

Emily Post is a registered trademark of The Emily Post
Institute, Inc.

EMILY POST'S ® FAVORITE PARTY & DINING TIPS. Copyright
© 2005 by The Emily Post Institute, Inc. Portions of this
material previously appeared in *Emily Post's Etiquette, 17th
Edition*. Copyright © 2004. All rights reserved. Printed in
the United States of America. No part of this book may be
used or reproduced in any manner whatsoever without
written permission except in the case of brief quotations
embodied in critical articles and reviews. For information,
address HarperCollins Publishers, 10 East 53rd Street,
New York, NY 10022.

HarperCollins books may be purchased for educational,
business, or sales promotional use. For information, please
write: Special Markets Department, HarperCollins
Publishers Inc., 10 East 53rd Street, New York, NY 10022.

FIRST EDITION

Printed on acid-free paper

ISBN-10: 0-06-0834595

ISBN-13: 978-0-06-083459-3

05 06 07 08 09 ❖/ WOR 10 9 8 7 6 5 4 3 2 1

Contents

INTRODUCTION

"Etiquette is the foundation upon which social structure is built. Every human contact is made smooth by etiquette, or awkward by lack of it."
EMILY POST, 1928

In an interview in *The American Weekly* in 1949, a reporter asked my great-grandmother, Emily Post, her opinion of a statement she had written nearly thirty years earlier in the landmark bestseller *Etiquette: The Blue Book of Social Usage*. It concerned the issue of a young woman traveling without a chaperone. "A young girl unprotected by a chaperone," wrote Mrs. Post, "is in the position of an unarmed traveler alone among wolves."

More than thirty years later, what did the *new, modernized* Emily Post think of her own advice? Preposterous, she said, "Imagine me writing anything like that! The world was different then, wasn't it?"

Today, it's easy to see what she meant: Our world, too, is vastly different than it was even a few years ago, and modern life can get awfully complicated. I am aware of this confusion firsthand, as I'm asked so many questions by people who want to know how to navigate new social situations and interact politely with each other in their everyday lives.

This handy pocket book is filled with practical tips that demystify these questions, such as how to graciously host a party without lots of stress; how to be a courteous, relaxed guest; and how to eat difficult foods with ease. Do you….Worry about giving a toast? Need to set a formal table, or know how to eat a lobster? Wonder about the right way to order wine, use a finger bowl, or deal with food spills? Wonder about how to mingle with people you don't even know? Want to throw a great party or be a good houseguest? Worry about committing a faux pas during a restaurant meal? My favorite tips for enjoying parties and managing a meal are all here in this guide—guaranteed to give you confidence for facing myriad situations as a host or a guest, whether at a casual get-together or a catered affair.

The answer to these many questions we face lies in applying the underlying principles of etiquette: respect,consideration, and honesty. These principles, in brief:

Respect. Respecting other people means

recognizing their value as human beings, regardless of their background, race, or creed. A respectful person would also never treat a salesperson, a waiter, or an office assistant as somehow inferior. Respect is demonstrated in all your day-to-day relations—refraining from demeaning others for their ideas and opinions, refusing to laugh at racist or sexist jokes, putting prejudices aside, and staying open-minded.

Self-respect is just as important as respect for others. A self-confident person isn't boastful or pushy but is secure with herself in a way that inspires confidence in others. She values herself regardless of her physical attributes or individual talents, understanding that honor and character are what really matter.

Consideration. Thoughtfulness and kindness are folded into consideration for other people. Consideration also encapsulates the Golden Rule: Do unto others as you would have them to do unto you. Being thoughtful means *thinking about* what you can do to put people at ease, while kindness is more about acts. Taken together, they lead us to help a friend or stranger in need, to bestow a token of appreciation, to offer praise.

Honesty. Honesty has more to do with ethics than

etiquette, but the two are intertwined. What could be more unmannerly than being deceptive? Honesty ensures that we act sincerely and is also the basis of tact: speaking and acting in ways that won't cause unnecessary offense. A tactful person can say something honest about a situation without causing great embarrassment or pain. In other words, tact calls for both empathy and benevolent honesty: "I like the stuffed mushrooms better" is honest, while "That dip tastes awful" may be equally true but amounts to an insult.

These three basic principles are universal and timeless. They haven't changed since Emily Post used them as the basis for her first book in 1922. They are the foundation for our actions today. Manners, on the other hand, are flexible. They change with the times and the customs of a specific place. Rather than thinking of manners as stiff, inflexible rules, think of them as guidelines to help us live according to the principles. This is as true in the world of entertaining as it is in other aspects of our lives.

As a seasoned guest and hostess of all manner of celebratory occasions, Emily Post didn't blink an eye when a fork was misplaced or a wineglass was the wrong size. What she considered unforgivable on the part of a host or hostess was neglecting to "do what is comfortable, both for those around you and for yourself." She also cringed if someone pointed out another person's shortcomings, especially in front of others. Instead, being respectful and kind, she said, is what matters; that's having good manners—nothing more, nothing less. I couldn't agree more. After all, the prime objective of a host or hostess is to make one's guests feel comfortable and welcome, not hold them hostage to a rigid set of tedious rules. The hosts are there to smooth any wrinkles and infect the occasion with the spirit of hospitality and generosity. What about being a considerate guest? Being an enthusiastic, willing participant is what it takes. Top those qualities off with being appreciative, and you're a guest who is eagerly asked back for more visits.

The best hosts spin magic out of thin air, creating the kind of special occasion guests can't stop talking about, while the best guests happily participate in the festivities. Who can forget that wonderful dinner party where you first tasted fresh oysters and sipped a special wine as you enjoyed warm conversation with old friends and new acquaintances? Who can forget the excitement of getting ready for an elegant affair, anticipating a night filled with possibility? Social occasions are filled with many such grand memories.

Wonderful times with friends and loved ones remind us that we are all a part of a larger whole. Whether you're with family, friends, business associates, or new acquaintances, just relax and apply plenty of kindness and respect. Surround each other in warmth and good cheer. The reward is often an unforgettably fine occasion, one indelibly etched in the hearts of all involved.

PEGGY POST
February 2005

Chapter One

TABLE MANNERS

Some people are so proficient at wielding eating utensils that they could teach a course in table manners. Many more are fairly comfortable with their table manners but feel they need to brush up on the finer points. Then there are those who feel uncomfortable to the point of dreading what could be seen as a mistake at a fine restaurant or a dinner party. Are they nervously overreacting? That depends. The world's not going to end because you don't know which fork to use or have no idea what to do with an artichoke. Then again, there are times when good table manners become vitally important. One instance is when you are taken to lunch by a potential employer who, for all you know, may be looking to gauge your overall finesse. (Legions of job applicants have missed being hired simply because they chewed with their mouths open or held the fork like a shovel.)

That's why it's a good idea to practice good table manners on a daily basis at the family dinner table or even when eating alone. When used routinely, table manners become second nature, lessening the chances of any missteps whether you're dining inside or outside your home. There are plenty of bonuses in not having to worry about concentrating on *how* you're eating—one being the opportunity to focus on the people with whom you're sharing a meal.

THE TABLE

It's easy to make sense of a traditional place setting—especially an informal one, which calls for only a few utensils. The basic rule: Utensils are *placed in the order of use*—that is, from the outside in. A second rule, although with a few exceptions: Forks go to the left of the plate, knives and spoons to the right.

The Informal Place Setting

When an informal three-course dinner is served, the typical place setting includes these utensils and dishes:

DINNER PLATE. This is the "hub of the wheel" and usually the first thing to be set on the table.

TWO FORKS. The forks are placed to the left of

plate. The dinner fork (the larger of the two) is used for the main course, the smaller fork for a salad or appetizer. Because at an informal meal the salad is usually served first, the small fork is placed on the outside at the far left.

NAPKIN. The napkin is folded or put in a napkin ring and placed either to the left of the forks or in the center of the dinner plate. (A folded napkin is also sometimes placed under the forks, though this makes diners go to the trouble of removing the forks before opening their napkins.)

KNIFE. The dinner knife is set immediately to the right of the plate, cutting edge facing inward. (If the main course is meat, a steak knife can take

An informal place setting

the place of a dinner knife.) The dinner knife could also be used for a first-course dish.

SPOONS. Spoons go to the right of the knife. A soupspoon (used first) goes farthest to the right, and a teaspoon (and sometimes a dessertspoon) between the soupspoon and knife.

GLASSES. Drinking glasses of any kind—wine, water, juice, iced tea—are placed at the top right of the dinner plate.

Other dishes and utensils are optional, depending on what is being served:

SALAD PLATE. This is placed to the left of the forks. If the salad is to be eaten with the meal rather than before or after, you can forgo this plate and serve salad directly on the dinner plate. However, if the entrée contains gravy or other runny ingredients, a separate plate for the salad will keep things neater.

BREAD PLATE WITH BUTTER KNIFE. If used, the bread plate goes above the forks, with the butter knife resting on the edge.

DESSERT SPOON AND FORK. These can be placed either horizontally above the dinner plate (the spoon at the top and its handle to the right; the fork below and its handle to the left) or beside the plate. If placed beside the plate, the fork goes on the left-hand side, closest to the plate; the spoon goes on the right-hand side of the plate, to the left of the soupspoon.

COFFEE CUP AND SAUCER. If coffee is to be served during the meal, the cup and saucer go just above and slightly to the right of the knife and spoons. If it is served after dinner, the cups and saucers are brought to the table and placed in the same spot.

The Formal Place Setting

The one rule for a formal table is for everything to be geometrically spaced: the centerpiece in the exact center, the place settings at equal distances, and the utensils balanced. Beyond these place-ments, you can vary other flower arrangements and decorations as you like. A formal place setting usu-ally consists of the following:

SERVICE PLATE. This large plate, also called a charger, serves as an underplate for the plate holding the first course, which will be brought to the table. When the first course is cleared, the service plate remains until the plate holding the entrée is served, at which point the two plates are exchanged.

BUTTER PLATE. The small butter plate is placed above the forks at the left of the place setting.

SALAD FORK. Unless the salad is to be served first, the small salad fork is placed at the left and closest to the plate.

DINNER FORK. The largest of the forks, also called the place fork, is placed to the left of the salad fork and is used to eat the entrée and side dishes.

FISH FORK. If there is a fish course, this small fork is placed farthest to the left because it is the first fork used.

DINNER KNIFE. This is placed to the right of the dinner plate.

A formal place setting

FISH KNIFE. The specially shaped fish knife goes to the right of the dinner knife.

BUTTER KNIFE. This small spreader is placed diagonally on top of the butter plate.

SALAD KNIFE. This knife, *if* provided, would be set between the dinner plate and the dinner knife. (Note: There is *no* salad knife in the above illustration.)

SOUPSPOON OR FRUIT SPOON. If soup or fruit is being served as a first course, the accompanying spoon goes to the right of the knives.

OYSTER FORK. If shellfish is to be served, the oyster fork is set to the right of the spoons; it is the only fork ever placed on the right.

GLASSES. These number four and are placed so that the smaller ones are in front. The water goblet is placed directly above the knives; just to the right goes a champagne flute; in front of these are placed a red- or white-wineglass and a sherry glass.

Knife blades are always placed with the cutting edge toward the plate.

No more than three of any implement is ever placed on the table (except when an oyster fork is used, in which case there are four forks). If more than three courses are served before dessert, the utensil for the fourth course is brought in with the food; likewise, the salad fork and knife may be brought in when salad is served.

Dessertspoons and forks are brought in on the dessert plate just before dessert is served.

HANDLING UTENSILS

Deciding which knife, fork, or spoon to use is made easier by the "outside-in" rule—using utensils on the outside first and working your way inward. If you find yourself confused (a utensil seems out of place, which could simply mean the salad is being served later), just wait to see what is served before choosing a utensil. Or watch the others at the table and follow suit.

How to Hold?

It's surprising how many people make a fist to hold their utensils, especially when the more comfortable alternative is the correct one: The fork or spoon rests on the middle finger of your hand, with your forefinger and thumb gripping the handle.

Do be aware that there are two different holding styles from which to choose: the American style (usually with fork tines up) and the Continental (or European) style (with fork tines down).

Is one style more proper than the other? Not at all. In fact, there's no reason not to use both during a meal: You might want to eat the meat Continental style and the other dishes American style. Use whichever is more comfortable.

The method for cutting food is the same for both techniques. Hold the knife in the right hand (or reversed, if you're left-handed) with your index finger pressed just below where the handle meets the blade. Hold the fork, tines down, in your left hand and spear the food to steady it, pressing the base of the handle with your index finger. As you cut food, keep your elbows just slightly above table level—not raised high and out.

How to hold a fork and knife while cutting food

Then come the differences in the two styles:

AMERICAN (OR ZIGZAG) STYLE. After the food is cut, the American method calls for placing (not propping) the knife on the edge of the plate, then switching the fork to your right hand before raising it, tines up, to your mouth.

American style of eating

CONTINENTAL STYLE. Once the food is cut, the knife is kept in your hand or laid across the plate as the other hand lifts the fork to your mouth. The fork is held tines down with the index finger touching the neck of the handle. The fork remains in the left hand.

Continental style of eating

Resting Utensils

Knowing where to rest utensils during and after the meal is important as well. First, never place a knife, fork, or spoon you've been using directly on the table; instead, place it diagonally on the edge of your plate.

When you pause to take a sip of your beverage or to speak with someone, place your knife and fork on your plate near the center, slightly angled in an inverted V and with the tips of the knife and fork pointing toward each other. (Don't worry about tines up or tines down, though it makes sense that the tines will face down if you're eating Continental style.) You may also rest your utensils in the American style, with your knife slightly diagonal on the top right rim of your plate and your fork laid nearby with tines up. These two resting positions, recognized by trained waitstaff, signal that you're not ready to have your plate removed.

At most restaurants, used utensils are replaced with clean ones for the next course. If, however, a waiter asks you to keep your dirty utensils for the

Two resting positions for utensils during a meal

next course (a practice apparently meant to cut costs), it's okay to ask for clean ones.

If soup or dessert is served in a deep bowl, cup, or stemmed bowl set on another plate, place your utensil(s) on this underplate when you finish. If the bowl is what is called a soup plate (shallow and wide), leave the spoon in the bowl.

At the end of the course, lay your knife and fork side by side diagonally on your plate (if your plate were a clock face, they would lie at four four o'clock); the knife blade faces inward, but the fork tines can be either up or down. This position not only serves as a signal to the server that you're finished but also decreases the chance that the utensils could fall to the floor when the plates are cleared.

Utensils indicating course is finished

Using Your Napkin

Be it cloth or paper, your napkin goes into your lap as soon as you sit down. The tradition has been for diners to wait until the hostess puts her napkin in her lap, but nowadays this custom is observed only at more formal meals. The significant word is "lap." Don't tuck a napkin into your collar, between the buttons of your shirt or blouse, or in your belt. (An exception can be made for the elderly or infirm; if someone is prone to spilling food, she has every right to protect her clothing.) Partially unfold the napkin (in other words, keep it folded in half), and don't snap it open with a showy jerk of the wrist.

Use your napkin frequently during the meal to blot or pat, not wipe, your lips. It's also a good idea to blot your lips before taking a drink of your beverage—especially if you're a woman wearing lipstick.

Put your napkin to the left side of your plate when the meal ends or whenever you excuse yourself from the table. Instead of folding or crumpling the napkin, just leave it in loose folds that keep any soiled parts out of sight. At the end of the meal, leave your napkin to the left or, if your plate has been removed, in the center of the place setting.

THE PARTICULARS OF SERVING

How a meal is served depends on its style. At a formal dinner, the food is brought to each diner at the table; the server presents the platter or bowl on the diner's left, at which point the food is either accepted or refused. (Alternatively, plates are prepared in the kitchen and then brought to the table and set before the diners.) At a more casual meal, such as an informal seated dinner party, either the host dishes the food onto guests' plates for them to pass around the table or the diners help themselves to the food and pass it to others as necessary.

Which way is food passed around the table when it is first served? Tradition says to pass counterclockwise (to the right)—but the point is for the food to be moving in only one direction. One diner either holds the dish as the next diner takes some food, or he hands it to the person, who then serves herself. Any heavy or awkward dishes are put on the table with each pass. Cream pitchers and other dishes with handles should be passed with the handle toward the person receiving them.

Serving Yourself

Your first concern when helping yourself to food is to pay attention to what you're doing and avoid spills. Then keep the following in mind:

➢ Gravy should be spooned directly from the gravy boat onto the meat, potatoes, or rice on your plate, whereas condiments, pickles, and jelly are put alongside the foods they're meant to accompany.

➢ Olives, nuts, radishes, or celery are placed on the bread plate. If no bread plate has been provided, put these items on the edge of your dinner plate.

➢ If the meal has started and something that would ordinarily be on the table is missing— salt and pepper, for example, or butter for the bread—mention it to the host only if you're certain it's an oversight: "Anne, is there any butter for the rolls?" Asking for anything else can be awkward and seem rude, especially at a dinner party. For one thing, the host might not have any steak sauce or pickle relish on hand; for another, requesting something additional suggests you think the food isn't up to par.

Refusing a Dish

When you're among friends, it's fine to refuse a dish you don't care for with a polite "No, thank you." At a dinner party where the host has gone to a great deal of trouble, it's good manners to take at least a little of every dish being offered.

If you're allergic to a food or on a restricted diet and your host urges you to help yourself to food you shouldn't eat, explain to her (not to the table at large) why you have no choice but to decline: "Sarah, shellfish is off-limits for me, but I'm sure all the other delicious dishes will more than make up for it."

DURING THE MEAL

Your first concern once the meal is served is when to start eating. Do you wait until everyone else's plate is full even as your food grows cold? Unless the meal consists of cold courses, your fellow diners (including the host, if any) will usually urge you to go ahead and start. If the group is large, begin eating once at least three of you have been given your food.

At a small table of only two to four people, it's better to wait until everyone else has been served before starting to eat. At a formal or business meal, you should either wait until everyone is served to start or begin when the host asks you to.

The other mealtime guidelines that follow are easy to digest. They're based on doing everything unobtrusively—the reason you shouldn't eat noisily, wave your fork in the air while talking, or snap a cloth napkin open instead of unfolding it.

Posture, Fidgeting . . . and Those Elbows

You needn't sit stiff as a rail at the dinner table, but hunching your shoulders over the plate (a posture often associated with using a fork like a shovel) is a definite "do not." Likewise, slouching back in your chair (which makes it look as if you're not interested in the meal) is not appropriate when eating with others.

As for not putting your elbows on the table, this drummed-into-us taboo applies only when you are actually eating. It's a different story when no utensils are being used; in fact, putting your elbows on the table while leaning forward a bit during a mealtime conversation shows that you're listening intently.

When waiting for the food to arrive or after the meal, you may want to keep your hands in your lap, if only to resist the temptation of fiddling with the utensils or other items. Refrain from drumming your fingers, jiggling your knee, or other fidgety habits, and always keep your hands away from your hair.

Cutting, Seasoning, and So On

As you begin and continue the meal, there are certain things you'll want to remember to do and others you'll want to avoid.

CUTTING FOOD. Cut your food into only one or two bite-sized pieces at a time. Doing this makes sense, since a plateful of cut-up food is not only unattractive but cools and dries out more quickly than food that is mostly intact. (The exception to the rule is when you help a young child cut his food.)

SEASONING FOOD. When at a dinner party or restaurant, always taste your food before seasoning it. Hastily covering a dish with salt or drowning it in ketchup implies that you think the cook's creation needs improving on.

CHEWING FOOD. Once you start to eat, don't literally bite off more than you can chew: Take a manageable bite, chew it well, and swallow it before taking another. Also remember that smacking, slurping, and collecting food in a ball in one cheek are major faux pas. When you have a mouthful of food, avoid two more things: taking a drink and talking. If you have more than a few words to say, swallow your food, rest your fork on your plate, and speak before you resume eating.

REACHING. Just how close does something on the table have to be before you reach out and get it yourself? That's simple: within easy reach of your arm when you're leaning only slightly forward. Don't lean past the person sitting next to you or lunge to perform what's known as the boardinghouse reach. A request to "please pass the [item]" is required for everything beyond that invisible boundary, as is a thank-you to whoever does the passing.

USING A FINGER BOWL. If you encounter a finger bowl (used either after eating a hands-on meal such as lobster or at a more formal meal when dessert is served), dip your fingers into the water and then dry them with your napkin. (See also Chapter 3, page 166: "Finger Bowl Finesse.")

Assorted Table Tips

➢ Remember to make good use of your napkin, wiping your fingers as necessary. Also use a small area of the napkin to blot your lips fairly often.

➢ If a piece of food keeps eluding your fork, don't push it onto the tines with your finger. Use a piece of bread or your knife as a pusher.

➢ Sop up extra gravy or sauce only with a piece of bread on the end of a fork; the soaked bread is then brought to the mouth with the fork.

➢ When you've finished eating, don't push your plate away from you. Nor should you loudly announce "I'm finished" or "I'm stuffed."

WHEN THINGS GO WRONG

Dealing with unexpected difficulties at the dinner table—from food that tastes off to a coughing fit to spotting a tiny critter inching along a salad green—is a concern for the polite diner. Such challenges can be managed with aplomb just by staying calm and keeping your sense of humor.

SPILLS. If you spill food on the table while taking it from a serving dish, neatly pick up as much as you can with a clean spoon or the blade of your knife; then wet a corner of your napkin in the water glass and dab the spot. If you knock over a drink, quickly set the glass upright and apologize to your tablemates: "Oh, I'm sorry. How clumsy of me! I hope none of it got on you." Get a cloth or sponge and mop up the liquid right away. In a restaurant, discreetly signal the server, who will put a napkin over any stains. In someone's home, immediately tell your host and help with the cleanup. (See also Chapter 2, page 90: "What Do I Do When . . .")

FOOD THAT'S TOO HOT OR SPOILED. If a bite of food is too hot, quickly take a swallow of water or another cold drink. If that's impossible or doesn't help, discreetly spit the scalding food onto your fork (preferably not into your fingers and definitely not into your napkin), and put it on the edge of the plate. The same goes for a bad oyster, clam, or any other food that tastes spoiled. Remove it from your mouth as quickly and unobtrusively as you can.

WAYWARD FOOD. Occasionally running your tongue over your teeth may let you know if you have a bit of food caught between your teeth. If the food stays put, excuse yourself from the table and remove it in the restroom.

If you notice food stuck in a fellow diner's teeth or on her face or clothes, you're doing a favor by telling her. If only the two of you are at the table, just say, "Millie, you seem to have a little something on your chin"; if you're in a group, it's better to silently signal Millie by catching her eye and lightly tapping your chin with your forefinger.

COUGHING AND SNEEZING. When you feel a sneeze or a cough coming on, cover your mouth and nose with a handkerchief or tissue—or your napkin, if that's the only thing within reach. (In an emergency, your hand is better than nothing at all.) If a coughing or sneezing bout is prolonged, excuse yourself until it passes.

Coughing and sneezing often lead to nose blowing. If you need to, excuse yourself and blow your nose in the restroom, being sure to wash your hands afterward.

CHOKING. If you choke on a bit of food and a sip of water doesn't take care of the problem, cover your mouth (if you can, though that would hardly be the time to worry about manners!) and dislodge the food with a good cough. Then remove it in the most practical way you can. If you have to cough more than once or twice, excuse yourself and leave the table.

Serious choking is another matter. If you find yourself unable to cough or speak, do whatever is necessary to get fellow diners to come to your aid. Thankfully, many people (and most restaurant personnel) are trained to perform the life-saving Heimlich Maneuver—a technique anyone will benefit from learning.

A QUESTION FOR PEGGY

I was a guest at a small dinner party last week, and I found a hair in a helping of potatoes au gratin. I didn't want to embarrass the hostess, but I couldn't bring myself to eat even a bite of the dish. No one said anything, but the hostess must surely have noticed my untouched potatoes. Should I have told her the reason once we were in private?

You get a gold star for not bringing it up, since finding a hair, that proverbial fly in the soup, or any other foreign object should either remain unmentioned until the time is right or not discussed at all. At a private dinner, you don't want to call the attention of the hostess or anyone else to the problem. You did your best in an awkward situation, and in the process saved the hostess any embarrassment.

If a foreign object isn't detected until you have it in your mouth, spit it quietly onto your fork or spoon and put it on the side of your plate. It's then up to you whether to continue eating the food or let it be.

FOOD-BY-FOOD ETIQUETTE

Facing unfamiliar or hard-to-eat foods or wondering whether the way you eat a particular food at home is "not done" in public is something that happens to most of us at one time or another. What you do depends on the situation. With friends, don't be embarrassed to say, "I've never eaten escargots before. Please show me how." If you're at a formal function or among strangers, just delay eating until you can take a cue from the other diners. Reviewing the guidelines below will help keep you from wondering what to do.

Apples and Pears

When served as part of a meal, an apple or pear is eaten with the fingers but is cut in quarters first (a paring knife is often set out for the purpose). Cut the core away from each quarter, then peel if desired.

Apricots, Cherries, and Plums

Eat an apricot, cherry, or plum with your fingers. To expel the pit, cup your hand over your mouth and push the pit forward with your tongue into your fingers. Then deposit the pit on your plate.

Artichokes

Artichoke leaves are always eaten with the fingers. Pluck off a leaf on the outside, dip its meaty base into the melted butter or sauce provided, then place it between your front teeth and pull forward. Continue leaf by leaf, placing discarded leaves on the edge of your plate (or on a plate provided for the purpose), until you've reached the artichoke's thistlelike choke or when the leaves are too small or meatless. Use your knife to slice off the remaining leaves and the choke, exposing the artichoke heart. Then cut the heart into bite-sized pieces and eat it with a fork, dipping each forkful into the melted butter or sauce.

Asian Dishes

The Asian cuisines most often encountered by Americans are those of China, India, Japan, and Southeast Asia (including Thailand, Vietnam, Korea, Malaysia, and Indonesia). Though there's no real need to follow the eating traditions from each country, it doesn't hurt to know a bit about them. For instance, at a Chinese or Japanese meal it's fine to hold the rice bowl close to your mouth; in Korean custom the bowl is left on the table. And then there are chopsticks, the use of which makes Chinese and Japanese food "just taste better" to many people.

It's also nice to follow the Asian custom of serving tea to your fellow diners before you fill your own teacup. (Traditionally, milk or sugar is added only to Japanese green tea, but there's no harm in doctoring any Asian tea to your liking.)

A meal at a Chinese restaurant is usually communal, with dishes being shared. All diners should have a say in what to order and then take equitable portions from the platters—even of the foods they like most. Near the end of the meal, don't take the last food left on a platter without offering it to the other diners first.

SUSHI AND SASHIMI. In Japan, the assorted raw fish dishes called sushi are eaten with chopsticks or the fingers. Whichever method you choose, there's a correct way to dip a piece of sushi into the accompanying soy sauce. So that the sticky rice won't break up, only the fish side is dipped into sauce; the piece is then brought to the mouth and eaten in one bite. If you forgo tradition altogether and use a fork, cut any pieces that are too large to eat in a single bite with your knife and fork.

A typical Japanese meal begins with sashimi—thinly sliced, raw, boneless fish served without rice. Before eating sashimi, diners mix a dollop of the green horseradish mustard called wasabi into the dish of soy sauce that is provided. The fish is then dipped into the sauce with chopsticks or a fork.

USING CHOPSTICKS

Chopsticks are used to eat Chinese, Japanese, Korean, and a few other Asian foods.

The first thing you should know is which end of the sticks to use. The food you're eating is picked up with the narrow end, while the broader end is used to pick up food from a communal serving plate. Once used, the small end of chopsticks should never touch any bowl or platter used by others.

A few more chopstick do's and don'ts . . .

Do decide which piece of food you want before you start in on an appetizer platter with your chopsticks. Poking the food as you decide what you want is a no-no, and once your chopsticks have touched a piece of food, you must take it.

Do bite in half dumplings and other small items that are a little too large to eat, holding the piece firmly in your chopsticks as you carefully bite.

Do raise your rice bowl to just under your chin when eating rice (unless you are dining in Korea, where all dishes remain on the table).

Do rest your used chopsticks on your plate or a chopstick rest, not directly on the table.

Don't pour any sauce over the food. Instead, use your chopsticks to dip a piece of food in the sauce (usually in your own small bowl) before raising it to your mouth.

Don't tap chopsticks on a dish to attract the attention of the server.

Don't grip the edge of a dish with chopsticks to pull it toward you.

Don't stick chopsticks upright in your rice bowl, rest them on the rice bowl, or transfer food to another diner's chopsticks. (These gestures are practiced only at Japanese funerals.)

Using chopsticks
Rest the lower chopstick on your ring finger, supporting it in the V of the thumb and forefinger. Hold the upper chopstick like a pencil, between the middle and index fingers and anchored with your thumb. Make sure the tips of the chopsticks are even. When you are picking up food, the lower chopstick remains still as the upper chopstick pivots, with your thumb as the axis.

Asparagus

When asparagus stalks are firm and aren't sauced, it's fine to pick them up with your fingers, one stalk at a time. (Asparagus is traditionally a finger food, and the English and many other nationalities still see it as such.) Think twice, however, about using your fingers for unsauced, firm spears if your fellow diners use a knife and fork or if you're a guest at a formal meal. When in doubt, use utensils.

Avocados

Avocado slices are cut and eaten with a fork. When an avocado is served halved, hold the shell to steady it and scoop out each bite with a spoon. When tuna salad or any other mixture is served in an avocado half, it's fine to hold the shell steady while eating the contents—this time using a fork.

Bacon

Eat fried bacon as a finger food when it is dry, crisp, and served whole. If the bacon is broken into bits, served in thick slices (as with Canadian bacon), or limp, eat it with knife and fork as you would any other meat.

Baked Potatoes (White and Sweet)

Baked white potatoes and sweet potatoes can be eaten in more than one way. The most common is to slit the top lengthwise with a knife, push on each end of the potato to open it wide, and mash some of the flesh with a fork. An alternative is to slice the potato clean through and lay the halves skin-down side by side.

Add butter, salt, and pepper (plus extras like sour cream, cheese, or bacon bits, if desired) and use your fork to mash the additions lightly into the flesh before taking a forkful from the shell.

Another method is to slice the potato in half lengthwise and use your fork to scoop the flesh of both halves onto your plate. Neatly stack the skins together on the edge of your plate and mix butter and any other condiments into the flesh with your fork.

If you like to eat the skin as well as the flesh, cut the potato into two halves and use your knife and fork to cut the potato and skin into bite-sized pieces, one or two at a time.

Bananas and Plantains

At an informal dinner, it's fine to peel a banana and eat it out of hand; just peel it gradually, not all at once. At a more formal dinner, follow your fellow diners' lead on whether to use fingers or fork. When a banana is eaten with a fork, the banana is peeled completely (the skin goes onto the edge of the plate) and cut into slices, a few at a time.

Raw plantains are eaten in the same way,

although these fruits are usually served fried and eaten with a fork.

Berries

Berries are usually hulled or stemmed before the meal, served with cream and sugar, and eaten with a spoon. Sometimes berries are served as or with dessert, or perhaps as part of breakfast. If strawberries are served unhulled, you can hold the berry by the hull to eat it; the hull and leaves then go onto the side of your plate.

Beverages

Beverages drunk at the table and at parties have a set of manners all their own, and some guidelines apply across the board: (1) Take a drink only when you have no food in your mouth; (2) sip instead of gulping; (3) if you're a woman, don't wear so much lipstick that your drinking glass will become smudged.

WATER AND ICE. Avoid the urge to gulp water at the table, no matter how thirsty you are. When drinking a beverage that contains ice cubes or crushed ice, don't crunch the ice in your mouth.

BEER AND SOFT DRINKS. When served at a meal, beer and soft drinks should be served in a mug or glass. Drink them straight from the bottle or can only at a picnic, barbecue, or other very casual occasion. (Good beers are often served in the bottle with an empty glass, which lets the drinker control how much he pours and the head on the beer.)

COFFEE AND TEA. Four quick don'ts: (1) Don't leave your spoon in the coffee cup or teacup or mug; place it on the saucer or a plate. (2) Don't take ice from your water to cool a hot drink. (3) Don't dunk doughnuts, biscotti, or anything else in your coffee unless you're at an ultracasual place where dunking is the norm. (4) Don't crook your pinkie when drinking from a cup—an affectation that went out with the Victorians.

When serving tea, note that a pot of freshly brewed loose tea tastes best; a second pot of hot water is used to dilute oversteeped tea and is poured directly into the cup. If using tea bags, put two or three bags in a pot of hot water and pour the tea when it has steeped. When putting a tea bag directly into a teacup or mug for steeping, allow it to drip briefly into the cup as you remove it (no squeezing it with your fingers or the string). Then place the bag on a saucer or plate.

What to do with empty packets of sugar and individual containers of cream? Crumple them and place them on the edge of your saucer or butter plate.

COCKTAILS. When you drink a cocktail, the only nonedible item you should leave in your glass is a straw; swizzle sticks and tiny paper umbrellas go onto the table or your bread plate. At parties, hold such accoutrements in a napkin until you find a waste receptacle.

If you want to eat cocktail garnishes like olives, cherries, or onions, by all means do. Garnishes on cocktail picks are easy to retrieve at any time, while those in the bottom of the glass should be fished out with the fingers only when you've finished the drink. (Think twice about eating an orange slice, since chewing the pulp off the rind is messy.)

WINE. See Chapter 2, page 83: "Ordering Wine"; Chapter 3, page 137: "Choosing and Serving Wines."

Bouillabaisse

To be enjoyed to the fullest, this seafood stew from Marseilles—made with varying combinations of white fish, clams, mussels, shrimp, scallops, and crab legs—requires using not only a soupspoon but also a seafood fork, knife, and sometimes a shellfish cracker. A large bowl should be placed on the table for shells. If no receptacle is provided, place empty shells on the plate under your soup bowl.

Bread

Before eating bread, use your fingers to break it into moderate-sized (not bite-sized) pieces. Then butter the bread one piece at a time, holding it against your plate, not in your hand. Hot biscuit halves and toast can be buttered all over at once because they taste best when the butter is melted. (See also "Butter," below.)

FRIED OR FLAT BREAD. The breads nan, papadam, poori (from India), and pita (from the Middle East) are brought whole to the table on plates or in flat baskets. Break or tear off a fairly sizable piece with your fingers and transfer it to your plate, then tear off smaller pieces to eat.

ROUND LOAF ON CUTTING BOARD. If a restaurant serves an entire round loaf of bread on a cutting board, use the accompanying bread knife to cut it in slices rather than wedges. Start at one side by cutting a thin slice of crust, then slice toward the center.

Burritos

See page 63: "Sandwiches and Wraps."

Butter

There are various ways to serve butter at the table: Place a stick on a butter dish with a butter knife;

slice a stick of butter and serve the pats on a small plate with a small fork (or on individual plates with little butter knives); or spoon whipped butter from a tub onto a small plate and provide a butter knife. When diners need to transfer the butter to their own plates and no communal utensil is provided, they use their own clean knives or forks. (See also page 54: "Olive Oil.")

When individually wrapped squares or small plastic tubs of butter are served in a restaurant, leave the empty wrappings or tubs on your bread plate (or, if no bread plate is provided, tucked under the edge of your dinner plate), not on the table.

Cantaloupes and Other Melons

Use a spoon to eat unpeeled cantaloupes and other melons that have been cut into quarters or halves. When melons are peeled and sliced, eat the pieces with a fork.

Caviar

Caviar is traditionally served in a crystal bowl on a bed of cracked ice. Use the accompanying spoon to place the caviar on your plate. With your own knife or spoon, place small amounts of caviar on toast triangles or blini. If chopped egg, minced onions, or sour cream is served, spoon the topping sparingly onto the caviar.

Cheese

When served as an hors d'oeuvre, cheese is cut or spread on a cracker with a knife. Provide a separate knife for each cheese so that the individual flavors won't mingle.

When cheese is served with fruit for dessert, it is sliced and placed on the plate with the fruit. Like the fruit, it is eaten with a knife and fork, not with the fingers.

When an after-dinner cheese course is ordered at a restaurant, the cheese will come arranged on plates centered with bread or crackers, a piece of fruit, or perhaps a small fruitcake of some sort. Cheeses served on bread or crackers are eaten with the fingers, but a knife and fork are used for everything on a plate holding cheeses and fruit or fruitcake (the cheeses are eaten separately so that the full flavor comes through). Start with the milder cheeses and progress to the strongest.

Cherries

See page 25: "Apricots, Cherries, and Plums."

Cherry Tomatoes

Except when served as part of a salad or other dish, whole cherry tomatoes are eaten with the fingers. But be careful: They're notorious squirters! It's best to pop the whole tomato into your mouth. If the tomato is too large to eat in one bite (as some varieties are), pierce the skin with your tooth or a knife before biting the fruit in half. When served whole in a salad or other dish, cherry tomatoes are eaten with a knife and fork after being cut with care.

Clams
See page 55: "Oysters and Clams."

Condiments
The perker-uppers we add to dishes—from salt and pepper to bottled sauces to relishes—have their own etiquette guidelines.

SALT AND PEPPER. Don't salt or pepper your food before tasting it, because assuming that the dish is well seasoned to begin with is an implicit compliment to whoever prepared it.

When someone asks for the salt or pepper, pass both. These items travel together, so think of them as joined at the hip. (Even a saltcellar is passed with the pepper.) If the shakers are opaque and you can't tell one from the other, the pepper shaker is the one with the larger holes.

At formal dinners, a saltcellar—a tiny bowl and spoon—sometimes takes the place of a shaker. You can use the spoon to sprinkle salt over your food as needed or you can fall back on the old tradition of placing a small mound of salt on the edge of your plate and then dipping each forkful of food into the salt. If no spoon comes with the cellar, use the tip of a clean knife; if the cellar is for your use only, it's fine to take a pinch with your fingers.

KETCHUP AND SUCH. At all but the most informal meals, serve ketchup, mustard, mayonnaise, and any other bottled sauces in small dishes. At picnics and barbecues, these condiments can come straight from the bottle.

Pouring steak sauce or ketchup over your food is fine if you're with family and friends or at a chain restaurant. But even the most avid bottled-sauce lover will probably have to do without at more formal dinners and tonier restaurants.

OTHER CONDIMENTS. Now that international cuisines are part of the American culinary scene, you're more likely to encounter several separate condiment dishes on the table. Spoon a small portion of the sauce or chopped-vegetable condiment onto the edge of your dinner plate or butter plate, replenishing it as needed. Never dip food directly into a communal condiment dish, and don't take anything from the condiment bowl directly to your mouth; it goes onto your plate first.

Corn on the Cob

Perhaps the only rule to follow when enjoying this handheld treat is to eat it as neatly as possible—no noisy nonstop chomping up and down the rows. To butter the corn, put pats or a scoop of butter on your dinner plate, then butter and season only a few rows of the corn at a time.

If no prongs for holding the cob are supplied, butter in a way that will keep your fingers from becoming greasy. Corn served at a formal dinner party should always be cut off the cob in the kitchen and buttered or creamed before serving.

Crab

When tackling a hardshell crab, start with the legs. Twist one off, then suck the meat from the shell; repeat with the second leg. Put the legs on the edge of your plate. To eat the body meat, use a fork to pick the meat from the underside.

A softshell crab is eaten shell and all, whether in a sandwich or on a plate. In the latter case, cut the crab with a knife and fork down the middle and then into bite-sized sections. You can eat the legs shell and all or pull them off and suck out the crabmeat inside; place any inedible parts on the side of your plate.

Cranberry Sauce
See page 38: "Condiments."

Cream Puffs
See "Desserts," below.

Crudités
See page 46: "Garnishes"; page 47: "Hors d'Oeuvres."

Desserts
What do you do with a dessert fork and spoon? Depending on what you're eating, these utensils are often interchangeable.

Eating pie or cake à la mode
Use a dessert fork and spoon: the spoon is used to cut and place a bite of pie or cake, plus a little ice cream, onto the fork. The dessert is eaten with the fork, with the spoon mainly being used as an aid.

In general, eat custards and other very soft desserts with a spoon, using the fork for berries or any other garnishes. Cake, pie, or crepes being served à la mode—i.e., with ice cream—may be eaten with either or both of the utensils. For firmer desserts such as dense cakes or poached pears, switch the utensils—the fork for eating, the spoon for pushing and cutting.

When you're served layer cake with the slice upright, turn it on its side with a dessert fork and spoon or any other utensil that remains at your place. If all of the other utensils have been cleared, then do your best with your fork and the fingers of the other hand. (See also page 48: "Ice Cream"; page 58: "Pastries.")

Empanadas

See page 62: "Quesadillas and Empanadas."

Escargots

Escargots (French for "snails") are baked or broiled and can be eaten in a number of ways. Shelled snails served on toast are eaten with a knife and fork. Escargots in a snail plate (ovenproof plates with indentations that keep unshelled snails in place while they are cooked in garlic butter and are being eaten) are usually grasped with snail tongs. Squeeze the handles to open the tongs, which will

Using snail (escargots) tongs

snap around the shell as you release the pressure.
The snail is removed with a pick, an oyster fork, or
a two-pronged snail fork held in your other hand.
The garlic butter that remains in the shells can be
poured into the snail plate and sopped up with
small pieces of bread on the end of a fork.

Fajitas

Fajitas (flour tortillas with a choice of fillings) are
filled and rolled by the diner, then eaten with the
fingers. To keep things neat, spread any soft fillings
(usually refried beans, guacamole, sour cream, or
melted cheese) onto the tortilla first, then add the
strips of beef, chicken, or seafood and top with any
garnishes. Roll up the tortilla and eat it from one

end. Your fork is used only to eat any filling that falls to the plate.

Figs

Whole figs can be eaten with your fingers at an informal dinner. If they are halved or are accompanied by prosciutto or a crumbly cheese, use your knife and fork.

Fettuccini

See page 56: "Spaghetti and other long noodles."

Fish

Fish as an entrée is often served as a fillet and eaten with a knife and fork. More daunting is a whole fish that you must fillet for yourself; it will most likely come with a fish knife and fish fork, tools designed for the job.

The first step is to anchor the fish with your fork and remove the head (placing it on a plate for discards). Then use the tip of your knife to cut a line down the center of the fish from gill to tail, just above the middle of the body. You can either (1) remove the skeleton at this point, lift the top half of the flesh with the knife and fork, and put it on the plate or (2) eat the flesh directly from the fish.

If you detect a fish bone in your mouth, work it to your lips unobtrusively; then discreetly push the bone onto your fork with your tongue and deposit the bone on the side of your plate.

Fondue

Eating fondue means sharing a bowl with others, so don't even think of "double dipping." When you spear a piece of French bread and dip it into the pot of melted cheese, hold the fondue fork still for a moment to let the excess drip off. Use your dinner fork to slide the cheese-covered bread onto your plate, then to eat it. The fondue fork is rested on your plate between dips. The same method applies to melted chocolate, a dessert fondue into which strawberries or cake squares are dipped.

Meat fondues require a few extra moves. When the bowl of cubed raw meat is passed, spoon several pieces onto your dinner plate. Spoon small pools of the sauces being served onto your plate. Firmly spear a piece of meat with your fondue fork and place it in the pot with the other diners' forks. When the meat is cooked, remove it and slide it onto your plate with your dinner fork. When it has cooled, cut it into smaller pieces to eat.

French Fries

When French-fried potatoes accompany finger foods like hamburgers, hot dogs, or other sandwiches, eat them with your fingers. At other times, cut them into bite-sized lengths and eat with a fork. Don't drown French fries in ketchup or other sauces. Instead, pour a small pool next to the fries and dip them in one by one, replenishing the sauce as needed.

Frog's Legs

Frog's legs can be eaten with either the fingers or a knife and fork. In the latter case, also use your knife and fork to move the inedible portions to the side of the plate.

Game Birds

See page 61: "Poultry."

Garnishes

Most garnishes aren't just for show. That sprig of parsley or watercress at the edge of the plate not only looks good but is tasty and nutritious. In all but the most informal situations, eat lemon slices or other citrus garnishes only if they are peeled and can be eaten with a fork. (See also page 34: "Cocktails,"; page 67: "Other garnishes.")

Grapefruit

Grapefruit should be served with the seeds removed and with each section loosened from the rind with a grapefruit knife. The rind, plus any seeds encountered, should be left on the plate.

Grapes

When pulling grapes off a bunch, don't pull them one at a time. Instead, break off a branch bearing several grapes from the main stem. If the grapes have seeds, eat them in one of two ways: (1) Lay a grape on its side, pierce the center with the point of a knife, and lift and remove the seeds. (2) Put a grape in your mouth whole, deposit the seeds into your thumb and first two fingers, and place the seeds on your plate.

Gravies and Sauces

Can you properly sop up gravy or sauce left on your plate with bread? Yes, but only with a fork. Put a bite-sized piece of bread into the gravy or sauce, sop, and then eat it using your fork Continental style (see page 10: "Continental Style").

Hors d'Oeuvres

At parties, you may be choosing hors d'oeuvres from platters set on a table or taking them from a passed tray. When taking more than two or three, use one of the small plates provided; anything less is held on a napkin. A napkin also goes under any plate you're holding so that you'll be able to blot your lips.

Take small portions from tables and trays and

avoid returning for plateful after plateful of food, which could make it look as if gobbling food is more important to you than socializing. Also remember not to eat, talk, and drink concurrently—one action at a time, please.

There is usually a small receptacle on the table or tray for used food skewers and toothpicks. If not, hold any items (including remnants such as shrimp tails and the swizzle stick for your cocktail) in your napkin until you find a wastebasket. Don't place used items on the buffet table unless there's a receptacle for the purpose.

When crudités (raw vegetables) or chips and dip are offered, spoon some of the dip on to your plate. When a communal bowl is used don't double dip—that is, never dip again with the same vegetable or chip once you've taken a bite of it. (See also Chapter 3, page 159: "A Dozen Dinner Guest Do's and Don'ts.")

Ice Cream

When you eat ice cream from a bowl, about the only misstep is to give into temptation and drink the meltage. Ice cream in a cone should be wrapped in a napkin to catch the inevitable drips.

You might want to take a cue from the old country when eating Italian ice cream, which is of two types: dairy ice creams (le crème) and fruit ices with no cream (le frutte). A serving typically consists of two or three scoops of different flavors, but Italians do not mix dairy and fruit types because the textures and flavors aren't complementary. (See also page 41: "Desserts.")

Kiwis

Use a sharp paring knife to peel away the fuzzy, inedible outer skin of a kiwi; then slice the fruit crosswise as you would a tomato. There's no need to remove the seeds, which are edible. Cut a slice into bite-sized pieces with your fork.

Lemons

Lemons are generally used as an accompaniment or garnish to other dishes. Cut a lemon into wedges, slices, quarters, or halves, depending on what it's being used for, removing the visible seeds. (See also page 46: "Garnishes.")

When squeezing a lemon section over a dish or into tea, shield other diners from squirts by holding a spoon or your cupped hand in front of the lemon as you squeeze. (Some restaurants fit lemons with a cheesecloth covering to prevent the problem.) The lemon is then placed on the edge of the plate (or saucer) or, in the case of iced tea, dropped into the glass if you choose.

Linguini

See page 56: "Spaghetti and other long noodles."

Lobster

A large paper napkin or plastic bib is provided for the lobster eater. Be sure to wear it, since handling this crustacean usually results in more than a few squirts and splashes. Holding the lobster steady with one hand, twist off the claws and place them on the side of your plate. Using the cracking tool (a shellfish cracker or nutcracker) that is typically provided, crack each claw (slowly, to reduce squirting) and pull out the meat with a fork or small lob-

Cracking a lobster claw

ster pick. You'll need to remove the meat from the tail (often already cut into two solid pieces) and cut it into bite-sized pieces.

Spear each piece of meat with your fork and dip it into the accompanying drawn butter or sauce before eating. (True lobster-lovers get additional morsels out of the legs by breaking them off one at a time, putting them into the mouth broken end first, and squeezing the meat out with the teeth).

A large bowl or platter should be provided for the empty shells. Finger bowls with hot water and lemon slices are often put at each place as soon as the meal is finished (see Chapter 3, page 166: "Finger Bowl Finesse").

Mango
Most varieties of mango are too large to be served individually. The fruit is usually divided so that the clingstone in the center can be removed. Because the skin is too tough to eat, the flesh is cut from it and eaten with a knife and fork.

Meats
A sizzling cut of meat can bring out the cave dweller in even the most well-behaved diner, but it's not always uncivilized to eat certain kinds of meat with the fingers.

CHOPS. At a dinner party or relatively formal restaurant, pork, lamb, and veal chops are eaten with a knife and fork. The center, or eye, of the chop is cut off the bone, then cut into two or three pieces. If the chop has a frilled paper skirt around the end of the bone, you can hold the bone in your hand and cut the tasty meat from the side of it. If there's no skirt, do the best you can with your knife and fork.

Among friends or at home, you can hold the chop and bite off the last juicy morsels of pork, lamb, veal. But if a chop is too big to be eaten with only one hand, it should stay put on the plate.

GRILLED MEATS. At an informal barbecue, hamburgers, hot dogs, ribs, and pieces of chicken are most enjoyed when eaten with the fingers. But sausages without buns are eaten with a knife and fork, as are fish, steak, and other meats served in large portions.

STEAK. Don't smother steak with steak sauce, especially when dining in a good restaurant. If you use a sauce, pour a small pool next to the steak and dip each forkful of meat before eating.

Melon

See page 36: "Cantaloupes and Other Melons."

Mints and Other Small Treats

When dinner mints, candy, petits fours, or candied fruits are offered in pleated paper wrappers or cups, lift them from the serving dish in the paper, transferring them to your plate before eating. Leave the paper on your own plate, not the serving plate.

Muffins

At the table, cut regular muffins in half either vertically or horizontally and butter the halves one at a time. (As with all breads, hold the bread on the plate—not in the air—as you butter it.) English muffins are split in half, and each side is spread with butter, jelly, honey, or marmalade.

Mussels

When eating moules marinières (mussels served in their shells in the broth in which they were steamed), remove a mussel from its shell with a fork, dip into the sauce, and eat it in one bite. Anywhere but a formal dinner, it's fine to pick up the shell and a little of the juice, then suck the mussel and juice directly off the shell. The juice or broth remaining in your bowl can be either eaten with a spoon or sopped up with pieces of roll or bread speared on your fork. Empty mussel shells are placed in a bowl or plate that has been put on the table for the purpose.

Olive Oil

When bread is served, a small, shallow bowl or plate of olive oil is sometimes set on the table instead of (or alongside) the butter. Either spoon a small pool of olive oil onto your bread plate or dip a bite-sized piece of the bread into a communal bowl of oil. Be sure not to double dip.

Olives

The olives on an antipasti platter are eaten with the fingers; you also use your fingers to remove the pit from your mouth while cupping your hand as a screen.

When olives come in a salad, eat them with your fork. If they are unpitted, remove a pit from your mouth by pushing it with your tongue onto the fork tip; then deposit the pit on the edge of your dinner plate.

Oranges and Tangerines

Eat these citrus fruits by slicing the two ends of the rind off first, then cutting the peel off in vertical strips. If the peel is thick and loose, pull it off with the fingers. Tangerines can be pulled apart into small sections before eating, while some varieties of oranges are more easily cut with a knife.

Seeds should be removed with the tip of the

knife, and sections are eaten with the fingers. The membrane around the peeled sections can also be removed with the fingers.

Oysters and Clams

Both of these bivalves are usually opened, served on cracked ice, and arranged around a container of cocktail sauce. Hold the shell with the fingers of one hand and a shellfish fork (or smallest fork provided) with the other hand. Spear the oyster or clam with the fork, dip it into the sauce, and eat it in one bite. Alternatively, take a bit of sauce on your fork and then drop it onto the oyster. If a part of the oyster or clam sticks to the shell, use your fork to separate it from the shell.

If oyster crackers are served and you'd like to mix them with your individual serving of sauce, crumble them with your fingers before mixing. Horseradish, too, can be mixed in, or a drop can go directly onto the shellfish if you like the hot taste.

When you order raw oysters or clams at an oyster or clam bar or eat them at a picnic, it's fine to pick up the shell with the fingers and suck the meat and juice right off the shell.

STEAMED CLAMS. Don't eat any steamed clams that haven't opened at least halfway; they may be spoiled. Open the shell of a good clam fully, holding it with one hand. If the setting is casual, pull out the clam with your fingers or a seafood fork. If the clam is a true steamer, slip the skin off the neck with your fingers and put it aside. Then, holding the clam in your fingers, dip it into the broth or melted butter (or both) and eat it in one bite.

If no bowl is provided for empty shells, deposit them around the edge of your plate. In a more casual setting, it's okay to drink the broth after you've finished eating the clams. In a more formal setting, follow the host's lead.

Papayas

These tropical fruits are served halved or quartered, with the seeds scooped out and discarded. The pieces can be either peeled and sliced—in which case they are eaten with a fork—or eaten from the shell with a spoon.

Pasta

Pasta comes in almost every shape under the sun, so it's not surprising that different forms are eaten in different ways.

SPAGHETTI AND OTHER LONG NOODLES. The traditional method for eating spaghetti, linguine, tagliatelle, and the like is to place the fork vertically into the pasta until the tines touch the plate, then twirl it until the strands form a fairly neat clump.

Twirling spaghetti

When the fork is taken to the mouth, neatly bite off dangling strands so that they will fall back onto the fork.

The alternative is to hold the fork in one hand and a large spoon in the other. Take a few strands of the pasta on the fork and place the tines against the bowl of the spoon, twirling the fork to neatly wrap the strands.

For those who haven't mastered the art of twirling pasta strands, there's the simple cutting method. Just be sure not to cut the whole plateful at one time; instead, use your knife and fork to cut small portions.

LASAGNA AND OTHER LAYERED PASTAS. With layered pasta dishes such as ziti and lasagna, a string of melted cheese can stretch from plate to fork to mouth with every bite. Cutting portions through with a sharp knife should prevent the problem.

PENNE, ZITI, AND OTHER TUBULAR PASTAS. Clumps of small-sized tubular pastas can be speared with a fork, while rigatoni and other larger tubular pastas should be cut into bite-sized pieces.

RAVIOLI. Small ravioli can be eaten in one bite, but standard squares (about 2 x 2 inches), should be cut in half with your fork. If you eat Continental style, push the bites onto the fork with your knife.

Pastries

Traditionally, a dessertspoon and dessert fork are used when eating such pastries as cream puffs and éclairs; the pastry is held in place with the spoon and cut and eaten with the fork. Bite-sized pastries such as rugalach are eaten with the fingers. The general rule? If you can't eat a pastry without getting it all over your fingers, switch to your utensils.

BREAKFAST PASTRIES. Croissants are eaten with the fingers. When adding jelly, preserves, or the like, carefully tear off small pieces and spoon on the topping.

➢ Danish pastries are cut in half or in quarters and eaten either with fingers or fork.

➢ Popovers are opened and buttered before being eaten (in small pieces) with the fingers.

➢ Sticky buns should be cut in half or in quarters with a knife and eaten with the fingers. If a bun is too sticky, use a knife and fork.

ÉCLAIRS. These cream-filled puff pastries are always eaten with a knife and fork. Just cut into them gently so that the filling doesn't squirt out. (See also page 41: "Desserts"; page 53: "Muffins.")

Peaches and Nectarines

Peaches are cut to the pit, then broken in half and eaten. If you don't like the fuzzy skin, peel the peach after halving it. When eating a nectarine (peeled or unpeeled, as desired), halve the fruit, remove the pit, and cut each half into two pieces.

Peas

To capture runaway peas, use your knife as a pusher to pile them onto your fork (held tines-up by necessity). Alternatively, use the tines of the fork to spear a few peas at a time. Never mash peas on the plate to make them easier to eat.

Pie

A slice of pie is cut and eaten with the fork, with the help of the dessertspoon if the crust is difficult to cut with the fork alone. When a slice of cheese is served with apple pie, it can be lifted with the fork and spoon, placed on top of the pie, and cut and eaten with each bite.

Pineapple

This rough and prickly tropical fruit is peeled, then sliced into round pieces and served on a plate. Use a dessertspoon and fork—the spoon for pushing the pieces, the fork for cutting and eating.

Pita Bread

See page 35: "Fried or flat bread."

Pizza

Take your pick: (1) Fold a pizza slice vertically at the center (to keep the toppings intact) and eat it with your fingers; (2) leave the slice on the plate and cut a bite-sized piece with a knife and fork. Deep-dish or Sicilian pizza, on the other hand, is normally eaten with utensils.

Plantains
See page 31: "Bananas and Plantains."

Plums
See page 25: "Apricots, Cherries, and Plums."

Popovers
See page 58: "Pastries."

Pork Chops
See page 51: "Meats."

Potatoes
See page 30: "Baked Potatoes (White and Sweet)"; page 45: French Fries.

Poultry
At a formal dinner, no part of a bird—be it chicken, turkey, game hen, quail, or squab—is picked up with the fingers. The exception is when a host encourages his guest to use fingers for eating the joints of small game birds served without gravy or sauce.

The no-fingers rule doesn't always apply when you're dining at home or in a family-style or informal restaurant. It's fine to eat fried chicken with your fingers and to do the same with the wings, joints, and drumsticks of other poultry. When eating a turkey drumstick, however, start with a knife and fork to eat the easily cut pieces of meat before you pick the drumstick up and eat the rest.

With the exception of a meal of fried chicken, there are certain situations in which utensils are always used. When eating the breast of a bird, use your utensils to cut off as much meat as you can, then leave the rest on the plate. Also use utensils when boneless poultry pieces are covered with sauce or gravy or are baked, broiled, or sautéed.

Quesadillas and Empanadas

When served as an appetizer, a quesadilla—a flour tortilla topped with a mixture of cheese, refried beans, or other ingredients and then folded and grilled or baked—is cut into wedges and eaten with the fingers. When served whole as a main course, it is eaten with a fork and knife.

Empanadas, which range in size from very small to quite large, are Mexican or Spanish turnovers filled with meat and vegetables. Small empanadas served as appetizers are finger food, while larger ones are eaten with a knife and fork.

Salad

When salad is served with a main course rather than before or after, it is best placed on a separate salad plate so that the salad dressing doesn't mix with any gravy or sauce.

Main-course salads—usually complete with pieces of chicken, shellfish, or cheeses and cold cuts—are put in the center of the place setting, just as any other entrée would be.

What about cutting up salad leaves? Large pieces of lettuce or other salad greens can be cut with a fork—or, if they're particularly springy, with a knife and fork. Just don't cut salad into smaller pieces all at one time.

Sandwiches and Wraps

Sandwiches more than an inch thick should be cut into halves or quarters before being picked up and held in the fingers of both hands—although a sandwich of any size can be eaten with a knife and fork. A knife and fork are always used for a hot open-faced sandwich covered in gravy or sauce.

WRAPS. Burritos, gyros, and other sandwiches in which the filling is wrapped in thin, flat bread (usually tortillas or pita bread) are most easily eaten with the hands. Any filling that falls to the plate is eaten with a fork.

Sashimi

See page 27: "Sushi and sashimi," under "Asian Dishes."

Seafood

See page 27: "Sushi and sashimi"; page 34: "Bouillabaisse"; page 40: "Crab"; page 44: "Fish"; page 50: "Lobster"; page 53: "Mussels"; page 55: "Oysters and Clams"; "Shrimp," below.

Shish Kebab

Shish kebab (chunks of meat and vegetables threaded onto skewers and then broiled or grilled) are eaten directly from the skewer only when they are served as an hors d'oeuvre. When eating shish kebab as a main course, lift the skewer and use your fork to push and slide the chunks off the skewer and onto your plate. Place the emptied skewer on the edge of your plate and use your knife and fork to cut the meat and vegetables into manageable pieces, one bite at a time.

Shrimp

Shrimp can be easy to eat or take a little work, depending on how they are served. The shrimp in a shrimp cocktail should be served peeled and are usually small enough to be eaten in one bite. The traditional utensil is an oyster fork, although any small fork will do. If the shrimp are bigger than one bite's worth, just spear each shrimp with your fork and cut it on the plate on which it's served.

Shrimp served as a main course are eaten with a knife and fork. When squeezing lemon over the shrimp, use your cupped hand or a spoon to shield other diners from squirts. If sauce is served in a separate bowl, dip your shrimp into it only if the bowl is yours alone; if the dish is communal, either spoon a small pool of sauce onto your dinner plate for dipping or spoon it over your shrimp. In some shrimp dishes, including garlic prawns, the shrimp are served unpeeled. Pick up a shrimp, insert a thumbnail under the shell at the top end to loosen it, then work the shell free. An extra plate should be provided to hold the discarded shells.

Shrimp served as hors d'oeuvres are eaten with the fingers. Hold a shrimp by the tail and dip it into cocktail sauce, if you prefer; just be sure not to double dip.

Snails
See page 42: "Escargots."

Soups
When serving soup, place the soup plates or bowls on an underplate—or on a saucer if cups are used. When the soup is finished or the spoon is laid down, the spoon is left in the soup plate, not on the dish underneath. If the soup is served in a cup, the spoon is left on the saucer.

HOW TO EAT SOUP. Hold the soupspoon by resting the end of the handle on your middle finger, with your thumb on top. Dip the spoon sideways into the soup at the near edge of the bowl, then skim from the front of the bowl to the back. Sip from the side of the spoon, being careful not to slurp. To retrieve the last spoonful of soup, slightly tip the bowl away from you and spoon in the way that works best.

If you want a bite of bread while eating your soup, don't hold the bread in one hand and your soupspoon in the other. Instead, place the spoon on the underplate, then use the same hand to take the bread to your mouth.

FRENCH ONION SOUP. This tricky-to-eat soup warrants its own guidelines. That's because it is topped with melted cheese (notorious for stretching from bowl to mouth in an unbroken strand) with a slice of French bread underneath. To break through to the soup, take a small amount of cheese onto your spoon and twirl it until the strand forms a small clump. Then cut the strand off neatly by pressing the spoon edge against the edge of the bowl; you could also use a knife or fork for cutting. Eat the clump of cheese and then enjoy the soup. If any strands of cheese trail to your mouth, bite them off cleanly so that they fall into the bowl of the spoon.

CRACKERS OR CROUTONS. If oyster crackers come with the soup, place them on the underplate and add a few at a time to your soup with your fingers. Saltines and other larger crackers are kept on the bread plate and eaten with the fingers. They can also be crumbled over the soup and dropped in, two or three crackers at a time. Croutons are passed in a dish with a small serving spoon so that each person can scatter a spoonful or more over his soup directly from the serving dish.

OTHER GARNISHES. Garnish soups with such optional toppings as croutons, chopped onions, or chopped peppers before you begin eating. With your clean soupspoon, spoon a portion from the serving dish and sprinkle it directly into the soup; you needn't place garnishes on your salad plate or bread plate unless you think you'll be wanting more. Put the serving spoon back on the garnish's underplate.

Spaghetti
See page 56: "Spaghetti and other long noodles."

Squab
See page 61: "Poultry."

Steak
See page 51: "Meats."

Strawberries
See page 32: "Berries."

Sweet Potatoes
See page 30: "Baked Potatoes (White and Sweet)."

Tacos
Crisp tacos are eaten with the fingers, since cutting the crisp shell with a knife and fork will leave it cracked and crumbled. Do use a fork, however, for any filling that falls to the plate. Soft tacos, topped with a sauce, are eaten with a knife and fork; unsauced soft tacos can be eaten with the fingers.

Tangerines
See page 54: "Oranges and Tangerines."

Veal Chops
See page 52: "Chops."

Watermelon
Serve no more than a quarter of a small watermelon at one time. At picnics and other informal affairs, you can hold the slice in your hands and eat it bite by bite. When using a fork, carefully flick the seeds away with the tines and push them to the side of your plate; then use the edge of the fork to cut bite-sized pieces.

TOP TEN TABLE MANNERS DON'TS

➢ Chewing with your mouth open or talking with food in your mouth

➢ Slurping, smacking, blowing your nose, or making any other unpleasant noises

➢ Holding a utensil like a shovel

➢ Picking your teeth at the table—or, even worse, flossing

➢ Failing to place your napkin on your lap or not using it at all

➢ Taking a sip of a drink while still chewing food (unless you're choking)

➢ Cutting up all your food at once

➢ Slouching over your place setting or leaning on your elbows while eating

➢ Executing the boardinghouse reach rather than asking someone to pass you something that's far away

➢ Leaving the table without saying "excuse me"

The important thing to remember is that all of the table manners described in this chapter help everyone—guest and host alike—act in a way that allows each diner to feel comfortable while having a the meal. These manners provide a sense of order. They are not a rigid set of rules, but instead have evolved over the years as the best way to easily and neatly facilitate eating various foods. If a diner makes a "mistake," the others at the table do not comment or point it out. Instead, they act in a way that demonstrates caring and consideration—the essence of good etiquette and the most important manner of all.

Chapter Two

EATING OUT

Part of the fun of eating out is the sheer variety of restaurants to pick from. We can tuck into barbecue with the kids at Jim Bob's Rib Shack or—when we can afford it—dine in the lap of luxury at the four-star Café Beaucoup D'Argent. Even those of us who live in the smallest cities are usually able to choose between a diner's meat-and-two-veggies menu and a sampling of ethnic cuisines. And as we enjoy ourselves, we won't have much more than basic table manners to worry about.

Right?

Not exactly. Understanding the place setting and not holding your fork like a shovel are only the starting points. How you interact with the waitstaff and other patrons—from hemming and hawing over the menu as the server waits patiently to letting your kids run free—can have a ripple effect that affects service for everyone. Of course, the more formal the restaurant, the more you'll have to watch your p's and q's. But most rules of good eating-out behavior apply as much at a coffee shop as they do at a white tablecloth-and-candles establishment.

RESERVATIONS OR NOT?

Unless you're the kind of person who loves to hang out at the bar while you wait for a table, reserving a table beforehand almost guarantees that you'll be spared frustration. It also enables you to specify any special seating preferences you might have beyond smoking or nonsmoking areas—a table in the garden, perhaps, or one in a quiet corner. If you're unfamiliar with the restaurant, there's another advantage: When you call to reserve a table, you can ask about any dress rules and which credit cards are accepted.

Some restaurants ask that you call to reconfirm your reservation a day or two ahead—and with good reason, given the number of thoughtless people who don't bother to cancel when their plans change. Not only is it an abuse of good faith to make a reservation and then fail to show up, but it could cost you money. Many restaurants, especially those in urban areas, ask for a credit card number when you reserve. If you don't cancel, you might be surprised to find a penalty charge appearing on your next bill.

If you're inviting one or more people as your guests, consider a few things before deciding where to reserve. First, find out if a guest especially likes or dislikes certain ethnic foods (simply ask when extending the invitation). You could also give the guest a choice of two or three restaurants. If you're hosting a group, pick a restaurant with a wide range of foods so that everyone present will find something to his taste.

Choosing a restaurant you know will help stave off problems. You may be eager to try the hottest new spot in town, but don't risk it unless you've been assured that it has quality food, good service, and the kind of atmosphere you seek.

ON ARRIVING

If you decide to use valet parking, you're about to have your first restaurant "etiquette encounter" — saying "thank you" to the attendant as she takes charge of your car. (Coming full circle, you'll reward a parking attendant with a tip when your car is returned.)

On entering the restaurant, your next encounter is with the person(s) standing behind the podium in the entryway: the maitre d', host, or hostess. Your behavior at this stage calls for little more than common sense: (1) Don't block traffic as you patiently await your turn, and (2) once you're face-to-face with the maitre d', smile and say "hello." If you've reserved a table, say, "We have a reservation in the name of Mullins"; if not, "We'd like a table for four in nonsmoking, please"—not "Table for four! And nonsmoking!" (Note: "Maitre d'," the term more often heard in upscale restaurants, is used in this chapter to avoid confusion with a restaurant patron who hosts others.)

If the restaurant has a coat check room, tradition says a man always checks his topcoat, while a woman has the choice of taking hers to the table. Packages, briefcases, umbrellas, and other items are usually checked; exceptions are folders of papers (often needed at a business meal), notebooks, or other small items. Rather than check their handbags, women normally take them to the table, where they're kept in the lap or at the feet—never on the tabletop.

What if your fellow diners arrive at different times? Here are some guidelines:

> ➢ The first arrival should wait for the second instead of being seated—unless, that is, arrangements to the contrary were made

beforehand or the restaurant is quickly filling up
(another reason for reserving a table in advance).

➣ When two of the group arrive together, they
should ask to be seated—either because they are
crowding the entry or they need to hold the
reservation until the others arrive. They should
also tell the maitre d' that others are coming and
ask him to direct them to the table. If the
restaurant's policy is to seat a group only when
all members are present, the early arrivals should
wait in the designated area or stand where they
won't impede the flow of traffic.

Being Seated

When the maitre d' leads you to a table, is there
any protocol involved? Only if you want to stand on
tradition. If a man and a woman are dining together, the "rule" is for the woman to walk directly
behind the maitre d', with the man following her;
in a mixed group, all the women precede the men.

Don't feel insulted if you're seated in a heavily
trafficked area, near an air-conditioner vent,
directly under a loudspeaker, or close by the
kitchen, restrooms, or door. At the same time, don't
hesitate to ask for another table when yours is less
desirable. Just stay calm and polite: "Could we be

seated a little farther from the door, please?" or "We'd prefer a table with a banquette if one is free." If you can't be accommodated, just grin and bear it if you made a reservation; if you didn't, you can say "thanks anyway" and try for a better table at another restaurant.

➢ If a group meal has an official host, it's the host's choice whether to direct guests to chairs. If he chooses not to, guests ask where they should sit.

➢ The better seats are those that look out on the restaurant or out a window onto scenery, not at a wall—something to keep in mind when you're hosting a meal or simply wish to give a fellow diner the better view.

➢ At a table with a banquette, women are traditionally seated on the banquette, the men on chairs opposite them.

➢ The host and hostess customarily sit opposite each other, and time was when couples were split up so that they would have a chance to chat with people other than their spouses. Today, seating choices depend more on the preferences of the group.

➤ A male guest of honor—say, a relative whose birthday or retirement is being celebrated—is traditionally seated at the hostess's right; a female guest of honor, at the host's right.

See also page 94: "Tips for Restaurant Hosts and Guests."

The Table Setting

At most of the more formal restaurants, only a service plate and a bread plate are on the table from the start. Small first-course and salad plates are brought out by the waiter as needed, then set on the service plate. (The service plate will be replaced by your plate of food when the waiter brings the main courses.)

Today even the most formal restaurants rarely set tables with every utensil under the sun. Flatware is usually kept to a minimum, with additional utensils brought out whenever ordered dishes require them. The most traditional place setting is the "outside-in," meaning that you start with the outermost utensils and work your way toward the plate. (See Chapter 1, page 2: "The Table.")

The usual glasses on a pre-set table are the water goblet and two wineglasses—the larger one for red wine, the smaller for white. At more formal restaurants, there may be additional glasses: the cylindrical champagne flute, which is better at keeping the wine bubbly than the saucer-shaped champagne glass of old; and a sherry glass, also cylindrical but smaller.

WAITERS ARE PEOPLE, TOO

Much of the success of your meal hinges on your interaction with your waiter or waitress. For better or worse, servers are quick to introduce themselves today—but even if they don't, a polite diner will treat them with respect. "Respect" doesn't mean thanking a waiter or waitress for every little task performed, but the occasional expression of gratitude is definitely in order. Treating a server as a robot is unforgivably rude, and an imperious or condescending manner shows you not as superior but small. In brief, do the following:

➤ Respond with a "hello" when the server first greets you, not a demand ("We need water!").

➤ Answer her questions with actual words, not grunts.

➤ Add "please" to your requests.

➢ Look at her as she recites the specials, and don't grimace if she describes something you don't like.

➢ Before you order, make sure everyone else at the table is ready to order.

➢ When you want your plate to be cleared, signal by placing your knife and fork in the "I'm finished" position—beside each other diagonally on the plate. (See also Chapter 1, page 11: "Resting Utensils.")

Call the server by catching his eye and giving him an expectant look. If he's some distance away, you can raise your hand to chin level, index finger pointing up. If he's looking elsewhere and isn't taking orders at another table, you can also softly call out "Waiter?" Snapping your fingers, waving your hand furiously, or addressing him by anything other than his name or "waiter" (or, in the case of a woman, "Mary," "waitress," "Miss," or "Ma'am") is less than polite. "Boy" and "honey" are permissible only if the waiter is your son and the waitress your wife. (See also page 108: "Paying the Bill.")

THE FINER POINTS OF ORDERING

Experienced restaurant-goers know that more than a little thought goes into ordering, from choosing pre-dinner cocktails to picking the meal courses to selecting the wines served during the meal. They also know how important it is to have made up their minds by the time they let the server know he can take their orders.

If you aren't ready, simply tell your server that you need more time. Holding him there as you keep changing your mind has repercussions: New arrivals at his other tables become impatient, some patrons have to wait longer to order, and the food your server is responsible for delivering to someone else must wait in the kitchen or under a heat lamp.

Two other important points:

➤ The signal that says you're ready to order is a *closed menu*. If you keep browsing the menu after you've decided what you want, how is the server to know?

➤ If those in your group want separate checks, make the request of your server at the start, even before you order a drink or appetizer. Asking for individual checks at the end of the meal slows down service for everyone in the restaurant because the server will have to spend time preparing them. Keep in mind that there's always the chance that a restaurant won't allow separate checks. If you plan to request them, find out if it's permissible by calling in advance or asking when you arrive.

Ordering Pre-dinner Drinks

It's fine to order beverages the first time the waiter asks, even if every guest at your table hasn't been seated; latecomers can order when the server returns with the first round. If there is a host, he can take charge and ask the guests what they would like. (See page 94: "Tips for Restaurant Hosts and Guests.")

Ordering Meals

Is it necessary to order the same number of courses everyone else does? Not really, especially when you're going Dutch. If you're the only one who orders an appetizer, you needn't ask the server to bring it with everyone else's main course—unless that's the extent of your meal; your companions have drinks, the bread basket, and conversation to occupy them until their dishes arrive. At a hosted meal, you should order an appetizer or first course or dessert when no one else does only at the host's urging.

Once you've narrowed down your choices, it's fine to ask your server which dish she recommends. When she recites a list of daily specials, it's smart to ask the cost of the dishes that interest you (specials are generally on the expensive side). If you're the guest at a meal, however, it's best to leave questions of cost to the host. (For menus without prices, see page 94: "Tips for Restaurant Hosts and Guests.")

It's fine to tell the server that you'd like to share an appetizer or dessert—and possibly even a main course if you know the servings to be huge. Just be sure to compensate the server with a more generous tip unless an "extra plate" fee is charged. She would have received a larger tip for two full meals, so you might want to keep that in mind when calculating how much to leave.

If you aim to have a leisurely conversation during the meal, order foods that can be eaten with ease. Lobster or crab in the shell, unboned fish, and pastas that may be messy or difficult to eat could make more demands on your time and concentration than you'd like. Also think twice about ordering a food that is unfamiliar to you. Unless you know how to eat an artichoke or tackle the crab claw in a bouillabaisse, stick with a dish that poses no unexpected challenges. (See also Chapter 1, page 25: "Food-by-Food Etiquette.")

Ordering Wine

Dinner wine is really a condiment for food, so it's best ordered after the menu choices have been made. The orderer (preferably the most qualified person at the table) can either choose a wine that goes best with the greater number of dishes or ask the advice of the server—or, in tonier restaurants, the wine steward (also called the *sommelier* or, if a woman, *sommelière*). Given the wide range in character of both red and white wines, the old rule that the former should be served with meat and the latter with seafood is a little musty. An easy alternative to a shared bottle is wine ordered by the glass, which allows the diners to match the wine with their meals.

When the server brings the unopened bottle to the table, he shows it to the orderer. If this is you, confirm the choice with a nod. The server then uncorks the bottle and pours a small amount of wine into your glass, which you sniff before taking a sip; a simple "That's fine" will let him know that the wine neither smells nor tastes off. (Briefly swirling the wine in the glass before sniffing releases its aromas—but making a show of the tasting procedure is best left to connoisseurs.) If you recognize the smell of a tainted, or "corked," wine, sniff the cork if the waiter hands it to you.

Otherwise, put the cork directly on the service plate or on the table.

The server pours the wine, serving the host or orderer last. (A diner who doesn't care to drink wine should either momentarily place her fingers over the glass when her turn comes or simply say, "No thanks"; turning the glass upside down is never the signal to use.) From that point on, it's up to the orderer to refill the guests' glasses if the waiter doesn't return to pour. White-wine glasses are traditionally filled three-quarters full; red-wine glasses, which are larger, are filled halfway.

A QUESTION FOR PEGGY

I know next to nothing about wine, but at a recent dinner for six the host insisted that I choose the wines. What should I have done? When you're put on the spot in this way, be honest: "I'd love to, but I know so little about wine, I think I should leave it up to you." What you should *never* do is fake it; otherwise, you could end up with a wine that doesn't fit well with the food. Don't be embarrassed about asking for help, since even alleged wine experts often know little about pairing wines with food. You could ask the server or the other guests for suggestions as you look over the list: "Which red do you think will go best with the dishes we're having?" Another tip: Don't think you have to order wine priced at the high end of the scale to get one of good quality.

START-TO-FINISH GUIDELINES

In all but the most informal restaurants, good manners require that you observe a number of civilities and procedures, from the proper use of your napkin and buttering your bread to enjoying your coffee and dessert.

Using Your Napkin

Put your napkin in your lap shortly after you sit down. As you use it, blotting or patting your lips is preferable to a washcloth-style wipe—and remember that this square cloth should never do double duty as a handkerchief. (For more on using napkins, see Chapter 1, page 14: "Using Your Napkin.")

When the meal is finished, traditional etiquette says you shouldn't place your napkin on the table until the host or hostess has done so, signaling the meal's end. The practice is largely obsolete, but remembering it may come in handy if you're in a group that leans toward formality. In any event, leave the napkin to the left of the place setting in loose folds, positioned so that any dirty part is out of sight.

Bread and Butter

If you want a piece of bread and the bread basket is close to your place setting, it's perfectly fine to pick up the basket and ask, "Bread, anyone?" After everyone has been served, pick out a piece and put it on your bread plate, along with a pat or two of butter. If the butter comes in a dish, use your butter knife to scoop out a portion to deposit on the edge of the bread plate. (The bread plate is also the place to put jam or jelly, as well as any finger foods served on a communal platter.)

Once you've taken a piece of bread from the basket, it's yours: Don't tear off a portion of a slice and then put the rest back in the basket. Put your bread on the bread plate. Each time you want some, break off one or two bites' worth, butter it while holding it on the plate (not in the air), and eat. Don't hold your bread in one hand and a drink in the other (the polite diner uses only one hand at a time), and don't take the last piece of bread without first offering it to others.

When an uncut loaf (with cutting board and knife) is placed on the table, the host—or whoever is closest to the basket—cuts three or four slices, leaving them on the board. If manageable, the board is then passed when diners want to cut their own.

First Courses

Appetizers are eaten with the small fork to the left of the dinner fork. If you're having soup, the server will probably bring the soupspoon with the soup; if it is already part of the place setting, it is to the right of the knife or knives.

If a platter for sharing has been ordered—say, of antipasti or stuffed mushrooms—it is passed around the table, with each diner holding it as the person next to him serves himself, using only the serving utensils provided.

Beverages

Before taking a sip of water, wine, or any other beverage, blot your lips with your napkin to keep the glass from becoming soiled. And remember that the water goblet is not a substitute for a finger bowl. If you want to clean your fingers, use your napkin—or, if a dish has been messy to eat, excuse yourself to clean your hands in the restroom if no finger bowl or hot towel has been provided. (See Chapter 3, page 166: "Finger Bowl Finesse.")

Main Courses

The period spent eating the main course is meant

to be enjoyable, but sometimes uncertainties or difficulties will creep in. Following are some of the problems that might crop up and tips for how to deal with them:

THE FOOD ARRIVES AT DIFFERENT TIMES. If a significant time elapses between the arrival of the respective diners' hot dishes, the host (or if there is none, the other diners) should urge the first who have been served to go ahead and eat. If everyone is having cold dishes, follow the rule of waiting until everyone is served.

YOU WANT TO SEND FOOD BACK. As a rule, send a dish back only if it isn't what you ordered; it isn't cooked to order (a supposedly medium-well fillet arrives bleeding, for instance); it tastes spoiled; or you discover a hair or a pest. Just speak calmly and quietly to the server when making the request. (See also page 94: "Tips for Restaurant Hosts and Guests.")

YOUR SIDE DISHES COME SEPARATELY. When vegetables are served in individual small dishes, it's perfectly proper to eat them directly from the dish. Or, if you choose to transfer the food to your dinner plate, use a fork or spoon to carefully slide them onto the plate. You could also ask your server to transfer the side dish to your plate when he brings it. If necessary, ask for the empty dishes to be removed so that the table isn't overcrowded.

YOU WANT TO TASTE ONE ANOTHER'S FOOD. Accepting another person's offer to taste a morsel of his dish—or offering a bite of yours—is fine as long as it's handled unobtrusively. Either pass your bread plate to the person so he can put a spoonful on it or (if he's sitting close by) hold your plate toward him so that he can put the morsel on the edge. Do not hold a forkful of food to another diner's mouth, and don't ever spear something off the plate of anyone else.

YOU'RE FACED WITH UNFAMILIAR FOODS. If a food you're not sure how to eat comes on a platter of appetizers—a type of sushi, perhaps, or crab in the shell—you, as a polite diner, have three choices of how to proceed: (1) Wait until someone else starts to eat and follow suit. (2) Ask how the food should be eaten (fingers or fork, for example). (3) Avoid the food altogether. Only the ill-mannered diner cries, "*Ewww* . . . what's that?"

YOU'RE NOT SURE HOW TO REST YOUR UTENSILS. During the meal, never place a fork or spoon you've been using directly on the table.

Instead, place the utensil diagonally on the edge of your plate, not propped against it like an oar. In fact, how you place your utensils on your plate is a code to the waiter, letting him know whether you have finished a course. (For resting utensils during and at the end of the meal, see Chapter 1, page 11: "Resting Utensils.")

Leftover Food

When you have food left over that you don't want to go to waste, it's usually acceptable to ask for a doggy bag—today, often a lidded container slipped into a small paper bag. When not to request one? First, at most business meals. (If you're dining with a business associate who's a close friend, it's fine to request a bag if you're going Dutch—but if she's the host, leave leftover food behind.) Second, at a wedding reception or other special function.

"What Do I Do When . . ."

It's the rare restaurant meal during which at least one spill or other perplexing glitch doesn't occur. These pointers will help you cope more easily.

I'VE DROPPED SOMETHING? Don't pick up a dropped utensil and put it back on the table. Tell your server, who will retrieve it and bring a replacement. The exception is when you drop utensils that might be stepped on or impede traffic around your table; in that case, act fast and pick it up yourself.

Likewise, if a napkin falls from your lap, ask your waiter for a replacement instead of fumbling around at your feet to retrieve it. Also inform the waiter if you've dropped food. If, say, a spoonful of ice cream falls to the floor, quietly tell the waiter at the end of the meal so that it can be cleaned up before the next diners are seated.

MY FORK OR GLASS IS UNCLEAN? Don't use your napkin to try to rub smudges off a utensil or glass. Also don't announce the problem to everyone—especially the host, if there is one. The next time a server stops by, discreetly ask for a replacement.

I SPOT A HAIR OR BUG? If there is a speck floating in your water or a pest or hair in your food, simply refrain from drinking or put down your fork until you catch the attention of the waiter. While it's probably impossible to keep the rest of the table from knowing something is amiss, try your best to avoid a fuss. If you want a replacement, you'll probably be served one fairly quickly. Regardless of how long your new dish takes to arrive, insist that your tablemates continue eating.

SOMEONE AT THE TABLE HAS FOOD ON HIS FACE? If you notice a speck of food on someone's face (or on a man's moustache or beard), subtly call the person's attention to it—a favor he will appreciate. Either say, "Oops, there's something on your cheek," or signal silently by using your index finger to lightly tap your chin or whatever part of the face is affected. As prevention for yourself, occasionally dab your chin and upper lip with your napkin to remove any wayward bits of food.

I HAVE SPINACH IN MY TEETH? Running your tongue over your teeth may let you know if you have a bit of food caught between your teeth, or one of your dining companions might discreetly let you know. If you can execute a quick wipe of your teeth with your napkin without attracting attention, do so. If the food won't budge, resist the temptation to dislodge it at the table with your finger or utensil; excuse yourself instead.

I KNOCK OVER MY DRINK? If you spill your beverage, immediately set the glass upright and apologize to all present: "Oh, I'm so sorry. That was so clumsy of me!" Don't feel as if you have to crawl under a chair; accidents happen to everyone. If the spill is wine (especially red), discreetly signal the waiter or a busboy, who will put a cloth over the stain.

THE WAITER TRIES TO WHISK MY PLATE AWAY?
If a server tries to take your plate before you've finished (maybe you've paused for a bit before taking that last bite of steak), don't hesitate to say, "Oh, I'm not finished," even if he's already on his way to the kitchen. If you *have* finished but don't want those who haven't to feel rushed, simply raise your hand slightly and say, "If you don't mind, please wait until everyone's finished before you clear the plates."

Condiments

Condiments range from salt and pepper to the individual small dishes that accompany Chinese, Indian, and other ethnic foods. For ways to handle these and other condiments, see Chapter 1, page 38: "Condiments."

A QUESTION FOR PEGGY

There seem to be so many things to dispose of during a meal—the paper on a straw, the little containers for butter, sweeteners, and jelly. Where am I supposed to put them?
It's simple. Just place the containers for butter and

jelly on the edge of the bread plate. Crumple any paper tightly and put it under the rim or on the edge of your bread plate or coffee saucer. The aim is to keep the table looking litter-free.

TIPS FOR RESTAURANT HOSTS AND GUESTS

In our more relaxed world, people who dine together think in terms of "hosts" and "guests" less often than they used to. But if you extend the invitation and it is understood that you're paying (as at many business meals), you're the host, like it or not. Today's hosts wear the mantle more lightly, but there are still a few things for them to consider—as there are for guests.

When You're the Host . . .

➢ Give careful thought to your choice of restaurant. Do the guests like exotic food or down-home cooking? Are they vegetarians or unrepentant carnivores? If you're hosting a group, choose a restaurant with enough menu choices to please everyone. (See also page 72: "Reservations or Not?")

➢ Reserve a table in advance. You may not mind

sitting at the bar waiting for a table, but others of your party may rather do anything but.

➤ Arrive a few minutes before your guests to relieve them of the worry of whether they should proceed to the table. If you wait at the table, give the maitre d' the names of the guests and ask her to direct them to you.

➤ If you wait in the foyer for several guests and some are more than ten minutes late, it's all right to go ahead and be seated, asking the maitre d' to show tardy guests to the table.

➤ As the host, you traditionally walk behind the guests if the maitre d' leads the way to the table. If she doesn't take the lead, you lead the guests. (See also page 75: "Being Seated.")

➤ If you're a woman, make clear to the maitre d' on your arrival that the check is to be presented to you and you alone—not to one of the men in a mixed group. Some women prefer to make advance arrangements for receiving the check (and sometimes for paying the bill).

➤ If a latecomer arrives after you're seated, stand as you extend your greeting.

➤ Whether you order a pre-meal drink or not, make it clear that your guests may order drinks, and of any sort.

➤ When ordering food, tell guests to feel free to order anything on the menu. Or get the point across by either recommending a dish at the middle or high end of the price range or telling them what you're having (again, a dish that is mid- to high-priced). Saying that a certain appetizer "looks delicious" lets guests know that you expect everyone to have a first course.

➤ If there's a lapse in the service and meals arrive at different times, urge those who've already been served to go ahead and start eating, especially if they are having hot food.

➤ If a mistake occurs—the wrong dish is brought to a guest, for example—tell the guest affected that you'll inform the waiter, then do so politely.

➤ When paying the check, don't display or disclose the total. Even a joking "Well, it's a darn good thing we enjoyed our food" could make guests feel they've ordered too extravagantly.

When You're a Guest . . .

➢ If you've arrived before the host and have taken a seat at the reserved table, it's best not to order anything other than water, especially if you're a guest at a business meal. When waiting for a close friend or family member, you might feel comfortable ordering a drink—but that's all.

➢ Never criticize the choice of table to the maitre d', no matter how much you dislike the location. The host alone should request a switch.

➢ When ordering a drink, try to stay somewhat in line with what everyone else orders. In a free-spirited group, tequila shots may not raise an eyebrow. But such choices are usually a bad idea if everyone else is having iced tea, fruit juice, and club soda.

➢ When your host orders a drink at a meal with a time limit (a business lunch or a pre-theater dinner, for example), order at least *some* kind of beverage so he won't think you're worried about pre-meal drinks slowing things down.

➢ As a general rule, don't choose the most expensive dishes on the menu, even if your host says, "Please don't hesitate to order anything you want." Try to order in the same general price range as the other guests. At the same time, don't feel you have to order the cheapest items on the menu, which could imply that you think that's all the host can afford.

➤ If there are no prices on the menu, keep from going overboard by remembering that some foods (pork, chicken, pasta, and rice-based dishes) are generally less expensive than others (beef, fish, shellfish, caviar, and anything that's served with truffles).

➤ If you need to send food back, do it only if there is really something wrong with it, not because you've decided you don't like it.

➤ Never complain about the food or service. Sounding dissatisfied could make it appear that you question the host's taste in restaurants.

➤ Even if the host has tipped the coat check person because he, not you, collected all the tickets on arrival, it's a nice gesture to try to reimburse him: "Jack, won't you please let me take care of this?"—but also know when to take no for an answer.

Fruit and Cheese

It's possible that a fruit course may be served at some point during the meal—either with the salad, after the main course (in that case, often with cheese), or as dessert. The days of peeling your own fruit are largely past, but a whole fruit should be quartered, cut up, and eaten with a knife and fork.

Cheese, seen on the menu in many upscale restaurants, is served before the dessert course. The server (a *fromager* [froh-mah-ZHAY] if male, *fromagère* [froh-mah-ZHEHRE] if female) will either bring a tray of cheeses or wheel out a cart, suggesting the most suitable choices. Slices of different types are then arranged on a separate plate (often centered with a piece of fruit, a wedge of fig, or plum cake) for each diner. While the cheese can be eaten on bread, the full flavor comes through if you eat it with a knife and fork. Start with the milder cheeses and progress to the strongest.

Dessert

In some place settings, a dessertspoon and fork are placed horizontally above the dinner plate. Use the fork for eating and the spoon as a pusher—or vice versa, depending on the softness of the dessert. (See also Chapter 1, page 41: "Desserts.")

Coffee and Tea

If a waiter places a pot of coffee or tea on the table but doesn't pour, the person nearest the pot should offer to do the honors, filling her own cup last. Two other points:

➢ Do not take ice from your water glass to cool a hot drink. Just be patient.

➢ Do not dunk doughnuts, biscotti, or anything else into your coffee.

For steeping and drinking tea, see Chapter 1, page 33: "Coffee and tea.")

Using Hot Towels

In some upscale restaurants, steamed hand towels are brought to diners at the end of the meal. Use the towel to wipe your hands and, if necessary, the area around your mouth. (Wiping the back of your neck or behind your ears is best not done in a restaurant.) Most waiters will take the towel away as soon as you've finished. If not, leave the towel at the left of your plate, on top of your loosely folded napkin.

WATCH YOUR STEP!

There are some behaviors that a restaurant patron should avoid as a matter of course. A few have to do with table manners and overall finesse, others with being considerate of everyone else. Even a smooth sophisticate who knows her place settings to a tee can come off as a boor to her companions and other patrons—not to mention the unlucky waitstaff—if she thinks only of herself. (For more on behavior while dining, see the chapter "Table Manners," page 1.)

Assorted No-no's

The first consideration is your posture. To show that you're alert and engaged, don't slouch. Sit up straight and don't stoop to eat your food. Also don't fidget with your tie or jewelry, drum your fingers, or jiggle your knee. A few other things to avoid:

SMACKING AND CRUNCHING. Eating as quietly as possible is essential to good table manners. For many, other people's smacking noises are as cringe-making as fingernails on a blackboard.

CHEWING SLOPPILY. Keep bites reasonably small and chew with your mouth closed. Don't form food into a ball in one cheek or take a sip of anything while chewing.

TALKING WHILE EATING. Make sure not to talk with even a little bit of food in your mouth; it doesn't take that long to swallow.

REACHING. Avoid the boardinghouse reach. Reach for something only within the invisible boundary that separates your personal space from the other diners'.

SOPPING AND PLATE-PUSHING. Using a piece of bread to sop up the sauce left over from a dish is fine—but only when the bread is speared by the tines of your fork. When you finish the meal, leave your plate exactly where it is: Pushing it away, even slightly, is a faux pas akin to the boardinghouse reach.

PICKING YOUR TEETH. Toothpicks should be used in private, not as you walk out of the restaurant or, worse still, at the table. Also refrain from noisily cleaning your teeth with your tongue at meal's end—an equally unattractive habit.

Dinner Conversation

Rule number one for socializing at the table: Don't talk so loudly that other diners become annoyed. The same goes for laughter, which escalates in proportion to the amount of alcohol being consumed. The occasional burst of laughter in a crowded restaurant is one thing, but repeated outbursts amount to disturbing the peace.

As you talk, sit up straight and don't fidget. And

choose your subjects with care. While politics, religion, and other potentially volatile topics aren't really off-limits, discussing them could risk nettling your dinner companions and putting a damper on the meal. Also avoid talking about anything bleak or unappetizing, including illness or surgery—two topics that are especially off-putting while people are eating.

The no-elbows-on-the-table rule applies only when you are actually eating, not conversing. Whenever your utensils aren't in hand, putting your elbows on the table and leaning slightly forward shows you're listening intently to what is being said—not to mention making it easier to hear in a noisy restaurant.

Another major concern: Turn off your cell phone from the moment you walk into a restaurant to the moment you leave. Indeed, more and more restaurants are requiring diners to either turn off their cell phones or switch them to vibrator mode. (See also page 109: "How Do You Spell 'Obnoxious'?")

TAKING THE KIDS

Restaurants that cater to children have become part of the American landscape, with birthday parties and children's entertainment the stock-in-trade of some national chains. At the other end of the spectrum are the high-end restaurants with quiet, formal settings, many of which don't allow children under age twelve. A good rule of thumb for parents is *not* to take young children to fancy restaurants; save that for when they're eight or nine and able to sit quietly at the table and practice good table manners.

Even in the most kid-friendly places, children should be taught to speak softly and to be on their best behavior when eating out. With some clear reminders and careful attention, eating out can be a good learning experience for children.

➢ Before going, remind your child of what's in store. She'll be given a menu, the waiter will take her order, and everyone will stay at the table until the meal ends.

➢ Since a young child probably isn't accustomed to waiting for meals, take a small drawing pad and colored pens (or other quiet playthings) to keep her occupied. Just be sure to put them away before the food arrives. For very small children, bring something they can eat while they wait for their order: packs of applesauce, crackers, individual servings of yogurt, and so on.

➢ Place your order as promptly as possible. For efficiency's sake, order for any child who's five or under. Be positive she knows what she wants before the waiter comes to take the orders. It disrupts service for the waiter to have to stand there while the child repeatedly changes her mind.

➢ If a toddler gets restless or noisy and you can't stop the disturbance, escort her from the dining area and stay with her until she calms down.

➢ Keep children seated in their chairs. If they run near servers who are carrying heavy, scalding-hot dishes, they risk harming themselves and others.

➢ If your child spills something or makes another mess, do whatever you can to clean it up. The less you occupy the busboy and waiter, the less you delay service for other diners. Because cleanup for your party will be larger than for those without children, be generous to the waitstaff with both your appreciation and your tip.

➤ If your child starts irritating other diners—say, by peering over the back of a booth or jumping—don't wait to put a stop to the behavior. (As obvious as that seems, it's amazing the number of parents who are willing to let mischief slide.) If the diner beats you to the punch (preferably with a polite "Excuse me. You probably don't realize it, but your daughter's jumping is shaking our booth. . . . Would you mind asking her to stop? Thanks."), apologize and say that it won't happen again. Then take pains to see that it doesn't.

➤ Know when to leave. Children find it hard to sit still for long periods, and it's unrealistic to expect them to. Unless dessert and coffee are served right away, you'll be wise to forgo them.

Excusing Yourself

When you need to get up to go to the restroom, it isn't necessary to say where you're going—a simple "Excuse me, please; I'll be right back" is sufficient. At other times, a brief explanation is in order: "Please excuse me while I check with the baby-sitter." Leaving without a word is rude.

When You Run Into Friends

If you happen to cross paths with friends at a restaurant, is it necessary to introduce them to your dining companions? If a friend or acquaintance drops by the table, the answer is generally no. If you want to talk briefly with the person, step aside before doing so. If, on the other hand, your intuition tells you that introductions all around are expected, by all means make them.

Unless they're sitting in a booth or on a banquette, where rising would be difficult, it's polite for both men and women to rise when someone is being introduced or has stopped by to talk; when the group is large, however, only those closest to the visitor rise. Traditionally, women did not rise for either sex, even if the visitor was elderly. Things are different now—especially at business meals, where anyone should stand briefly for introductions.

If you run into friends while being seated, don't conduct a lengthy conversation with them while the rest of your party sits down and begins to peruse the menus. You don't have to sit immediately, but do tell your tablemates that you'll "be there in a minute"—and then keep your word. Likewise, don't say you're leaving the table for "just a minute" to visit someone else and then stay away so long that the people at your table feel shunned.

Grooming at the Table

In most circumstances, it is more polite to excuse yourself and put on lipstick in the ladies' room than to do it at the table. The exception is when the restaurant has an informal atmosphere and you're among friends, in which case you can apply the lipstick quickly. What you should avoid is a primping routine—no compact, no powder. And then there's that never-to-be-broken rule: Whether you're a man or a woman, don't use a comb at a restaurant table, nor should you rearrange your hair or put your hands to it wherever food is served. Using dental floss at the table is a major never-ever. Believe it or not, some people have no qualms about doing something so private in public.

PAYING THE BILL

If you're hosting a meal, it's a good idea to let the maitre d' or waiter know in advance that the check should be given to you, lest an eager guest try to pay it himself. (Note to guests: Don't take the edge off the host's hospitality by trying to grab the check. Your turn will probably come.)

HOW DO YOU SPELL "OBNOXIOUS"?

Less-than-desirable behavior is magnified in a restaurant because paying patrons have rightful expectations of a relatively tranquil meal. Here are some acts to avoid at all costs.

Holding court on a cell phone. Even though you'd think that the diner who gabs away on his cell phone would be an extinct species by now, he's still hanging on. As pitiful as he is (trying to transmit the message "I'm on the go, I'm a deal-maker, I'm *connected*" while appearing just the opposite), he's responsible for a serious disruption. To everyone's misfortune, he's never heard of the rule that says there's a time and a place for everything.

Bribing the maitre d'. People who charge to the front of the line in a busy restaurant and flash a large bill at the maitre d' insult not only the restaurant management but whomever they've just pushed past. A tip for a maitre d' who has given you a good table and attentive service is acceptable (it's usually given on leaving), but trying to buy a good table is inexcusable.

Flaunting your wealth. A noisy table of big-spending revelers flaunting their riches by ordering bottle after bottle of exorbitantly priced wines (not to mention puffing away on cigars) is one of the worst kinds of showing off. There's no excuse for such behavior, no matter how large one's bank account.

Getting soused. The table in the corner that periodically explodes with laughter, whoops, and hollers that almost startle other diners out of their chairs is either listening to the funniest person on earth or drinking too much. In a calm setting, few things irritate restaurant patrons more than the tipsy table that erupts in a rafter-rattling roar.

Taking over. Groups celebrating a special occasion sometimes seem to think they've rented a private room. They tie balloons to chairs, stand on chairs to make speeches, and toast whomever in full cry—to the chagrin of everyone present.

Overdoing displays of affection. A romantic candlelit dinner for two is undoubtedly the time for a bit of cooing and moony gazing, but couples who paw each other or kiss passionately are hard to ignore. The prohibition on this sort of behavior falls under the umbrella of respecting the right of other patrons not to be distracted from their own pleasurable dining experience.

When the check comes, keep it out of view as you look it over. It's not a guest's business to know what the cost of the meal came to — nor your obligation to disclose it. When you're ready to pay, signal the waiter by putting the check holder to the edge of the table, with the bills or the credit card sticking out a bit.

Going Dutch is another matter. Splitting the bill can be approached in two ways. First, you each pay only for what you ordered; second, you split the bill in equal shares even though the cost of the food isn't even-steven. The latter is preferred by many because it's simpler, and friends don't usually mind if some pay a little less than their share. There may be times, however, when you feel like you're subsidizing the others (they shared two bottles of wine and you had none; they had steak and you had a dinner salad). If you feel you're overpaying more often than you should, don't be afraid to say you'd like separate checks; just make sure to ask before ordering, for both your fellow diners' and the server's sake: "Hope nobody minds, but I'm going to have to ask for a separate bill tonight." Putting the shoe on the other foot, it is incumbent on those whose orders were disproportionately large to insist that they put more into the kitty.

If you're paying cash and want the server to keep

the change, tell her so directly. Saying "Keep the change, thanks" will prevent the server from standing in line at the cashier for no reason.

COMPLAINTS . . . AND APPRECIATION

Restaurateurs can tell you that keeping diners happy is one big job. They also point out that people are much more likely to voice their complaints than their appreciation. That's not to say that you shouldn't let it be known when the service is slow, a server is rude or careless, or the food comes badly prepared. The restaurant depends on its customers' approval for its livelihood, and its faults can't be corrected unless they're brought to the management's attention. Make a complaint quietly, without attracting the attention of other diners. Speak first to whoever committed the error. If he makes no effort to correct the situation, take your complaint to the manager or captain.

Rudeness and laziness might be reported, but don't confuse them with the inability to serve too many people. Often, a server works as hard and fast as possible but still can't keep up with patrons' requests. If this is the case, you could still complain to the management, but be careful not to put the blame on the server, who's undoubtedly no happier about the situation than you are.

If after making a legitimate complaint you receive no satisfaction at all, you might reduce the tip (or, in the most extreme cases of bad service, leave none) and avoid that restaurant in the future.

On the other side of the coin, appreciative comments and a generous tip are more than welcome when you're pleased with the service. While tips are expected, comments like "The food couldn't have been better" or "The service was especially good" are a pleasant surprise and mean a great deal to someone who is trying to do her best. The management will also appreciate hearing from a customer who is satisfied and doesn't hesitate to say so.

BUFFET RESTAURANTS, DINERS, ETCETERA

The advantage of a buffet restaurant is that you can sample as many foods as you like. It is also slightly more economical because your tips to the staff are smaller.

Because you're permitted to make as many trips to the buffet as you wish, there's no reason to overload your plate. Also, leave your first plate and utensils on the table for the waiter or busboy to remove. Health codes in many states don't allow dirty dishes to be taken back to the serving stations, since soiled utensils and plates could spread germs . . . and besides, clean plates look more appetizing.

Cafeterias

When a cafeteria is crowded and there are no empty tables, it's fine to take an empty chair at a table already occupied—but only if you ask, "Is this seat taken?" or "Do you mind if I sit here?" Diners who join a stranger are under no obligation to talk, but it's all right to start a casual conversation if the other person seems receptive.

Diners, Coffee Shops, and Delicatessens

Most diners and coffee shops have both booths and tables served by waitstaff, while delicatessens often have tables for customers but no table service. At diners and coffee shops, all the guidelines for dining at a regular restaurant apply.

At a deli, you usually place your order and then either pick it up or wait until a counter person delivers it. The customer clears the table and disposes of paper plates and plastic utensils on leaving. No tips are expected in this case.

Fast-Food Establishments

The etiquette you should observe in these most casual of restaurants boils down to treating those who serve you with respect. That means not directing your attention solely to your companion(s) or your cell phone conversation as you order and pay (especially at a drive-through) and handing your bills and change to the server instead of putting the money on the counter. And a "please" and "thank you" are essential.

Two other tips: Save time for everyone in line by deciding what you want to drink before you order, especially when a drink comes with a meal package. And when ordering at a drive-through window, be sure to drive your car close enough so that the server won't have to strain his back when he hands over your food.

Chapter Three

THE DINNER PARTY

Interesting people, good food, and a pleasant setting are the ingredients. What brings them together to make a great dinner party? Not champagne and caviar, not fine china and silver—though these are certainly gracious embellishments. The indispensable elements are the hosts and the spirit they bring to the occasion.

Many years ago, Emily Post wrote, ". . . if the enthusiasm of your [the hostess and host's] welcome springs from innate friendliness—from joy in furthering the delight of good-fellowship beneath your own roof—you need have little doubt that those who have accepted your hospitality once will eagerly look forward to doing it again and again." Her advice is as fresh today as it was in 1922, just as her prediction that "perhaps in time the term formal dinner may come to mean nothing more exacting than company at dinner" has proved correct.

The very formal dinner party, though still a staple for ceremonial and certain business events, has given pride of place to informality. The etiquette of today's dinner party owes much to the casual style of family meals. Rigid rules have been replaced by flexibility, and today's successful hosts are more concerned with the needs of their guests than the perfection of their table settings. Whether a seated meal with candlelight and professional servers or a grab-a-plate-and-serve-yourself cookout, a great party is always grounded in enthusiasm and friendliness.

But you can't throw a party on good intentions alone. Even the most casual get-together requires careful organization, thoughtful execution, and courteous manners. Although primarily devoted to the etiquette and intricacies of hosting a dinner party, this chapter is also intended to guide dinner party *guests* and maximize everyone's enjoyment of the occasion.

THE FIRST STEPS TO A SUCCESSFUL PARTY

Fun as it may be to dream up a scrumptious menu and think about whom you will invite, first things must come first—when you will hold the party, how many guests you'll include, and how much money and time you're prepared to spend. These businesslike basics will largely determine all other decisions.

Date and Time

The time of your party is up to you, but be conscious of local customs and work schedules, particularly if the party will be on a weeknight. Consider time changes; a party might begin a little later during daylight savings time, a little earlier during the darker months.

Consult your own calendar and be attuned to what is going on among your likely guests. A conflict with religious services, a major sport or cultural event, or parents' night at the neighborhood school can cause problems. Check with a guest of honor before setting a date (or with a family member if the party will be a surprise). If you plan to hire help, keep in mind that experienced cooks, servers, and caterers are usually booked well in advance for holidays as well as graduation and wedding season.

The Guest List

All sorts of things might go awry during the evening, yet your party can be a rousing success—with the right guest list. The key is to invite people whom you like and have every reason to believe will be interested in each other, whether they already know one another or are strangers.

The mix of guests will largely determine the *personality* of your event—peaceful, relaxed, intense, spirited. If you want a tranquil evening, don't include guests who are likely to bicker. You can ask your ardent Republican friend to this dinner and your equally vehement Democratic friend to your next gathering. But if you and your other guests enjoy lively political discussions, invite both.

Sometimes, the occasion itself will dictate all or part of your guest list—dinner for business associates and their spouses, members of a club or an organization, a guest of honor (in which case the guest is often asked to suggest people whom he or she would like to include), or family members. When entertaining people you don't know well, especially at a large party, it's a good idea to include a sociable friend or two who will be willing to help you keep the evening running smoothly.

There's no foolproof formula for the guest list. And few hosts have escaped the classic party poopers—the nice guy who becomes a buffoon after one cocktail, the quiet type who decides to flirt outrageously, the egotist who has to have the spotlight, the sloppy eater. Managing difficult guests is, for most people, a matter of learning through experience, and experience comes through doing. Don't be discouraged if an occasional gathering doesn't go according to plan; every party is a chance to learn and hone your hosting skills.

PARTIES WITH A THEME

Themed dinner parties can be loads of fun. But if too obscure, too cute, or too difficult, the theme can fall flat. An obscure theme is one that guests simply don't get or don't care about. Decorating in the colors of your alma mater may delight guests at an alumni reunion but can bewilder or go unnoticed by those who have no reason to make the connection. "Too cute" includes themes that are childish, inappropriate to the guest list, or overdone. For example, it's traditional to serve green beer at a St. Patrick's Day dinner, but coloring food green can put guests off their meals. A theme is too difficult when its execution consumes too much of the hosts' time, energy, and often their budget. Whether as subtle as decorating with seasonal flowers or as elaborate as a Halloween party with everyone in full costume, a good theme is one that all guests will appreciate and enjoy.

How Many Hosts?

Co-hosting is an excellent way to throw a large dinner, which may be too expensive for an individual or couple. Bonding together with friends is also a good way to host events honoring others—graduation, engagement, wedding, anniversary, birthday, promotion, and retirement dinners.

Co-hosts should get together at the outset; discuss dates, guest list, budget; and decide who will do what. Duties should be divided as fairly as possible, taking advantage of each person's skills and interests. If one of the hostesses has a great eye for color but can't boil water, she's the obvious choice to do the centerpiece—not the crown rib roast. Co-hosts also share hosting responsibilities, including greetings and introductions, kitchen duty, and serving or supervision of hired servers.

The host at whose home the party will be held has the greatest responsibility, and others should offer to assist with cleaning in advance of the event as well as post-party cleanup. Supplementing the "home host's" tableware and kitchen equipment is another way to pitch in. Sometimes a co-host can't physically help (often the case with an elderly or infirm person or someone who lives out of town). But able-bodied people who are too busy to contribute their time should think twice before co-hosting.

How Many Guests?

Most people can handle intimate dinners for four to six people; entertaining larger numbers depends on your ability to accommodate everyone comfortably. Take an objective look at your house or apartment and picture it with your guests present. Where will they sit? Is there plenty of room for people to move about freely and eat in comfort? If your dinner table is designed for eight, then inviting twelve for a seated meal will mean cramming. Pity the people who will be stuck at the corners of the table, and invite fewer guests or opt for a buffet.

Do you have plenty of comfy seating for before and after the meal? What about bathrooms? Too many guests and too few facilities can cause lines. Do you have enough plates, glasses, utensils, and table linens for the number of people you want to invite, or are you prepared to purchase, borrow, or rent the necessary items?

Experienced hosts take everything into account, including the weather. Thirty people may be optimal for a buffet in the warm months, when guests can overflow onto the porch or terrace. But the same number may be too many to confine inside in the dead of winter.

Budgeting Money and Time

A successful dinner party is one that seems almost effortless but has been planned with military precision. One of a host's first steps is budgeting, so decide how much you can spend on the evening; account for everything, down to the last swizzle stick. It's better to trim your supply list at the beginning than to overspend on decorations and then be forced to nickel-and-dime on food and beverages.

Wise hosts and hostesses budget their time as carefully as their money. One person or a couple can manage a small casual dinner, but assistance of one kind or another is usually needed for eight or more at a seated dinner and for larger groups at a buffet. Do you have family members or friends who can help with cooking and service? Would it be a good idea to hire one or several servers, kitchen assistants, or bartenders for the evening? Or is professional soup-to-nuts catering the best way to go? (See page 127: "The Catered Affair.")

Cooking and serving are only part of a host's responsibilities. If you're stuck in the kitchen or preoccupied with getting the meal on the table, who will greet your guests, make introductions and keep conversation going, and spot little problems before they become big ones? Hosting a dinner party is a good example of multi-tasking, so decide which tasks you can handle and which require help.

ADVANCE PREPARATIONS

With the day and time, guest list, and budget decided, you're ready to plan exactly how to organize the evening. For many hosts, this is the best part of preparation—calling for equal parts of creativity and common sense.

The Dining Format

No matter how formal or casual, there are two basic formats for dinner parties—the seated meal and the buffet—but each allows for a good deal of variation.

SEATED DINNER WITH FOOD SERVED AT THE TABLE. Guests are seated at the dining table. The food is brought to them, or serving dishes and platters are placed on the table and passed. The meal is served in courses, and plates are changed between courses. The number of courses can range from two to six, and the level of formality is entirely up to the hosts. (See page 163: "The Formal Dinner Party.")

ALTERNATIVES TO DINING AT HOME

Hosting at a restaurant or club is often the only way that very busy people can entertain. It enables them to give parties in distant locations, making arrangements by phone and e-mail, or to entertain on a larger scale than is possible in small apartments and condos. It's also a great way to reciprocate those who have hosted you when you don't have the capacity for at-home dinner parties. If you worry about cost, consider all the expenses of an at-home party, plus your time; your actual expenditure for dining out may be the same or even less.

The first steps of planning are the same as for an at-home affair: deciding on the date, the guest list, and how much you want to spend. Then scout for a place if you don't have one in mind; consult with proprietors; settle on menu, seating arrangements (you may want to book a private room or terrace seating), and type of food service (seated or buffet, with or without bar service); and organize the method of payment, including gratuities. Unless you're familiar with a restaurant or club, sample the cuisine before making a final commitment.

SEMI-BUFFET, OR SEATED DINNER WITH BUFFET SERVICE. The meal is eaten at the dining table and perhaps smaller tables set for dining, but the food and plates are put out on a separate buffet table or tables, and guests serve themselves. Drinks, dessert, and sometimes the salad course may be brought to the guests at their tables. Semi-buffets adapt beautifully for outdoor parties with seating at patio or picnic tables.

BUFFET WITH CASUAL SEATING. This is the true buffet. Guests serve themselves at the buffet and then sit where they please in the party area—living and dining rooms, family room, patio. A buffet requires adequate seating and table space (coffee table, side tables, and tray tables), so diners will have a place for glasses and cups and saucers. Casual buffets include barbecues, pool parties, and box suppers.

COCKTAIL BUFFET. A cocktail buffet is basically a cocktail party (see Chapter 5, page 203: "The Return of the Cocktail Party") at which the food is sufficient to constitute a meal. The menu is more extensive and heartier than hors d'oeuvres, and food can be eaten with the fingers only or with no more than a plate and fork. Food is put out buffet-style on one or more tables, and guests take items at their leisure. A cocktail buffet often begins later than a conventional cocktail party—6:30 or 7:00 pm—and lasts two to three hours. A *cocktail reception* is the most formal type; the party is usually in honor of a person or event, and the dress is often black tie for men and fancy cocktail or evening dresses for women.

The Catered Affair

Caterers can be lifesavers for busy hosts, and catered meals are often less expensive than people imagine. But finding and hiring just the right caterer requires a considerable investment of time. If you've never hired a caterer, ask family and friends for recommendations, or check out local business listings. Search carefully, meet personally with prospective caterers, and check every detail before signing a contract.

A caterer who comes to your home offers *off-premises* services. *On-premises* catering is done at the caterer's location—hotel, club, restaurant. Some caterers do both, so you might ask your favorite restaurant if they also cater off-premises or can suggest someone.

➢ Before calling caterers, establish your budget; the date, time, location, and format of the party; and the approximate number of guests. Think about what you want the caterer to do—full meal and bar preparation and serving, food preparation only, all food or just part of the meal. Do you want the caterer to supply plates, dinnerware, and glasses? Some caterers also offer furniture rental, table linens, and decorations and flowers.

➢ If you don't have a specific caterer in mind, meet with several and get more than one estimate. Caterers usually give average per-person estimates, but you can ask for an itemized list that breaks out food, serving personnel, and equipment costs. Does the estimate include tax and gratuities? How is payment to be made? Discuss the menu in detail and inquire about your options. Consider the labor involved in food preparation and serving. Paying careful attention to specifics can save you from unpleasant surprises when the final bill is submitted.

➢ Some caterers will come to your home for an interview. If not, you should be clear about your facilities and possible limitations such as a small kitchen or difficult access for catering vehicles. If the dinner will be at a clubhouse, on a boat, or at some other site away from your residence, describe the place and its location clearly.

➢ Check references. Be certain the caterer is properly licensed and has a valid catering permit. Check the caterer's insurance (general liability and liquor liability) and workers' compensation coverage. Your state or local health department has information about licensing requirements in your area.

➢ Visit the caterer's kitchen. Most caterers offer samples of their cooking, so taste the cuisine. You can ask to see photos of catered meals to get a sense of the caterer's presentation style.

➢ Determine whether the caterer is able to be flexible—for instance, if meals can be provided for any guests whom you know have special requirements, such as kosher or vegetarian meals.

➢ Finally, you should have a comfortable professional relationship with the catering service you hire. The caterer and his or her helpers will be working in your home, and even if they handle everything, you should oversee the work so that it's done to your satisfaction.

Inviting Your Guests

Although casual dinners may be arranged at the last minute, invitations to a dinner party are normally issued a week or two before the event—three to six weeks if the occasion is formal or the social calendar is crowded. In general, the more formal a dinner, the earlier invitations are mailed, since guests need time to prepare for an elegant evening.

The formality of the event usually dictates the nature of the invitation. For very formal dinners and cocktail receptions, invitations are printed, engraved, or handwritten. Invitations to less formal dinners can be printed to order, pre-printed cards with information filled in by hand, handwritten notes, or issued by phone or in person. E-mail is a possibility as long as the invitees are regular e-mail users.

Phoned or in-person invitations are often a must for events like a potluck supper when guests are expected to contribute food and other items, though you might follow up with an attractive invitation.

Invitations to seated dinners and small buffets usually include an RSVP because the host needs to know exactly how many people to plan for. A notation of "Regrets only" or no request for a reply may be fine for a large buffet-style dinner; as long as you have an approximate number, there's usually plenty of food for a few extra people. But an RSVP will give you the most accurate guest count.

In addition to date, time, place, names of the hosts, and RSVP, an invitation should indicate the nature of the party and any other pertinent information, including directions to the party location if needed.

DETERMINING THE MENU

Your menu will depend on the formality or informality of your party, whether food is served at the table or buffet, who will be doing the cooking, the tastes of your guests, and your budget. Also consider the size of your kitchen and how it is equipped and ventilated. If you have one oven, for instance, you won't be able to bake or roast everything, so include dishes that can be cooked or warmed on your cooktop as well. You also need adequate cold storage and freezer space for items prepared in advance.

A good dinner menu is a balance of richness and simplicity. For example, a first course of a heavy soup or shellfish in a cream sauce might be balanced by an entrée of roast beef au jus or chicken baked in fresh herbs. A sauced entrée might be accompanied by crisp, lightly seasoned vegetables. Everything should complement everything else; flavors should enhance flavors. Too many sauces or "sweet" items can be overwhelming. Consider food textures, colors, and aromas.

Envision the full plate you will set before your guests. Will it appeal to the eye and nose as well as the taste buds? For inspiration, today's cookbooks, cookery magazines, and their Internet versions often include sample menus as well as recipes.

If you're the chef, ask yourself what you do well. A basic rule of cooking for a group is to avoid experimenting. You'll feel more confident preparing foods that you are familiar with, and it's usually easier to adapt recipes you know than to try something totally new.

Many people think that a dinner party menu has to include more courses than a family meal, but that isn't necessarily the case. A formal dinner menu traditionally comprises five or six courses, but most at-home dinner parties consist of three or four, and in some cuisines (Asian and Indian, for instance), a main course and dessert are more than adequate.

AN ELABORATE FORMAL DINNER MENU can include as many as six courses:

1. Soup, fruit cup or melon, or shellfish
2. Fish or sweetbreads (often omitted if shellfish is served first)
3. Entrée, or main course (usually roast meat or fowl with vegetables)

4. Salad
5. Dessert
6. Coffee and cordials (with fresh fruits and/or cheeses
   served after dessert as an option)

Note that salad is served *after* the entrée, contrary to the U.S. restaurant practice of serving salad first. The reason is that fresh greens and salad vegetables in vinegar-based dressings are served to cleanse the palate between the meat course and the dessert and dessert wine. Traditionally, wine is not served with the salad course because the vinegar in the dressing will interfere with the taste of a good wine.

If a light sorbet is served between courses, it is also intended to clean the palate. The serving is small, and diners may have a taste or eat it all.

AN AT-HOME DINNER PARTY MENU is often limited to a starter course (soup, fruit, a vegetable or shellfish dish, pasta), entrée, and dessert, with coffee after. Salad can be served as a starter or accompany the entrée.

A BUFFET DINNER MENU may eliminate the starter course, though the host will often provide more than one entrée and a greater variety of side dishes. Buffet-style dessert sometimes includes more than one sweet plus fresh fruit for diners who prefer a lighter end to the meal. You might set a separate table featuring several desserts or a single, spectacular creation such as a tiered cake. Dessert plates, forks, and spoons are put on the dessert table.

A COCKTAIL BUFFET MENU may include hors d'oeuvres or just a hearty spread of foods that can be eaten while guests stand. Napkins are essential, since finger food is often eaten directly after being taken from trays or containers. Toothpicks and skewers are provided for fruit wedges, meatballs, chicken wings, and other foods that are sticky or greasy. (Put out an empty plate or bowl, so guests can dispose of used skewers and bones.) Crackers, toast points, and flat breads serve as bases for meats, pâté, and flavorful spreads. If plates and utensils are needed, usually dessert plates and forks are sufficient.

Dietary Considerations

If you know that a guest follows a special diet but aren't sure of the specific restrictions, don't hesitate to call and ask. It's especially wise to inquire if the guest is the only one (or one of a few) whom you're inviting. There are also some precautions a host or cook can take without consulting guests.

RESOURCES FOR THE COOK

Thanks to the wealth of resources available today, preparing party meals is easier than ever, and even inexperienced cooks can put together wonderful dinners for groups. Supermarkets and sometimes the corner grocery offer prepared foods, from deli fare to whole roast turkeys and baked hams. Check out the produce department for washed salad greens, and the freezer section for cooked entrées. The average mall includes gourmet stores, ethnic markets, and specialty food and beverage shops. Even small towns probably have a bakery and perhaps an independent butcher who will cut meats to order (a great find for kitchen novices who pale at cookbook instructions like "butterfly" and "fillet paper-thin"). If you don't mind the shipping costs, you can put together an entire party meal with food catalogs, a credit card, and a telephone.

Many dishes can be completely or partially prepared in advance and refrigerated or frozen. The time saved on party day is a blessing, and some dishes actually improve after a day or two. Recipes today often include information about advance preparation and proper storage as well as nutritional content.

One is to avoid cooking with peanuts, peanut oil, and additives such as monosodium glutamate (MSG) that commonly cause allergic reactions. Another is to steer clear of very hot or heavily spiced dishes unless you know your guests enjoy them. If you serve a highly spiced dish, also provide a blander alternative for guests who can't take the heat.

In general, a guest with dietary restrictions should *not* alert his host ahead of time—except when he's the only guest or one of a few. When the restrictions are due to allergies, other medical conditions, or religious sanctions, it's especially important to inform the host. A vegetarian may also say something if he's the only guest. He can offer specifics. For example, does he exclude red meats only or all meat, fish, and fowl? Are eggs and dairy products, including cheese, off the list? Whatever the dietary restriction, the thoughtful guest should offer to bring his own food to a small gathering or when visiting overnight with a relative or good friend.

At a large gathering, a guest with food restrictions should eat what he can, though it's imperative that he ask the host if he has questions about any off-limits ingredients. When asking, he should take the host aside so that others won't think there might be something wrong with the food. Some people with allergies and other food restrictions simply eat something before attending a dinner party to ensure that they won't be hungry if there isn't much served that they can eat.

When a dietary "restriction" is simply a matter of taste, the guest makes his preferences known only if his host asks ("Do you eat meat?" or "Do you like Brussels sprouts?"). It's rude for a guest to inquire about a party menu just to see if he'll like what's being served.

Choosing and Serving Wines

For those who aren't wine connoisseurs, purchasing and serving wine may seem like crossing a minefield. But people have been making, drinking, and enjoying wines for millennia, without the wine snobbery that sometimes crops up today.

Trust your taste buds. If you think a wine tastes good with a certain food, your guests will probably agree. Try to find a wine shop with knowledgeable staff who can make recommendations based on your menu and your budget. (Very good wines need not be expensive or rare; purchasing by the case can save money.) Food and wine publications offer useful suggestions, but try to sample a wine you don't know, preferably with the food you plan to serve. Keep a record of wines and brands you particularly like for future reference.

You don't have to serve a different wine with every course, but even with the most casual dinner, it's nice to have a white (perhaps for cocktails and first course) and a red, as long as the wines go with the food.

The following fundamentals should help with wine selection and service—and eliminate some misconceptions.

RED AND WHITE. Traditionally, white wines are served before red, and dry ("sec") wines before sweet. But the food more often determines the choice of wine. For instance, a somewhat sweet wine may be particularly suited for a rich, sweetish entrée such as lobster.

Red wine with red meat and white wine with fowl and fish remains a serviceable guideline, but the specific food is a better way of deciding which wine to serve. In general, wines should be comparable to the food in "body" or "weight" (relative strength), so that one doesn't overpower the other: robust wines with hearty dishes, lighter wines with more delicate fare. The variety of wines today is so great that color is no longer a predictor of strength.

UNCORKING. Wine is usually uncorked about a half hour before being served in order to aerate, or "breathe." Wine is generally opened, tasted, and allowed to air—and corks are sniffed for vinegary or "off" smells—in the kitchen. Champagne is often opened, with care, at the table and served as soon as the cork is popped.

TEMPERATURE. Generally, white and pink wines are chilled before serving; red wines are not. But the old rule of serving reds at room temperature was made back when room temperatures tended to be colder than in modern housing, so a red wine may benefit from slight chilling. Any wine that is too cold or too warm loses its distinctive flavor. Your wine dealer can provide temperature guides, but again, trust your instincts and your taste.

Between pourings, a chilled wine can be returned to the fridge or kept in an ice bucket on a side table. For serving, the bottle is usually wrapped in a large dinner napkin or white towel to hold the chill and prevent dripping from condensation.

DECANTING. Aged red wines and port wine develop sediments, so they are decanted—poured into a glass container or carafe—to separate the clear wine from the sediment. The bottle is stored upright for twenty-four hours; then the wine is carefully poured into the decanter until the sediment reaches the top of the bottle. To catch stray bits, you can pour through cheesecloth. Other wines can be poured into carafes simply because it is an attractive way to serve.

POURING. At the table, wine is poured before each food course if there's a new wine for that course. This gives the diner a chance to smell and taste the wine on its own. Traditionally the host pours for women and older guests first, then the men, and fills his or her glass last. At a buffet, however, wine is offered when a guest is seated or set out on the drink table for guests to serve themselves.

➢ Wineglasses are filled approximately halfway, though sparkling wines are often poured to the two-thirds level so the drinker can enjoy the bubbles. Filling a wineglass near the rim makes it difficult to savor the aroma, and a full glass is easier to spill.

➢ Still wines are poured into the center of the glass, but sparkling wines are poured against the inside of the glass (tilt the glass slightly) to preserve the natural carbonation. To prevent drips, give the bottle a *slight* twist to end pouring.

HOLDING THE GLASS. Since white wines are normally chilled, a white-wine or champagne glass is held by the stem to prevent the transfer of heat from the hand. Red-wine glasses, which are sometimes larger and a bit heavier, may be held by the bowl. The bowl of a cognac glass is cupped in the hand because cognac benefits from warming. This also explains why cognac and brandy glasses are not made of cut crystal, which interferes with the warming.

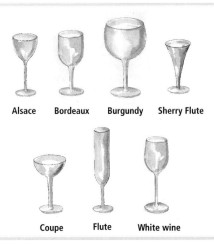

Alsace   Bordeaux   Burgundy   Sherry Flute

Coupe   Flute   White wine

A QUESTION FOR PEGGY

I have a number of friends who rarely or never drink alcohol (several are recovering alcoholics) and others who, like me, enjoy mixed drinks and wine with dinner. I always find myself worrying about how to make everyone happy when I entertain.

First, be sure to stock your bar with a variety of nonalcoholic beverages: soft drinks, still waters, flavored waters, soda water and tonic, fruit juices, iced tea. Then serve nonalcoholic drinks just as you do wines and spirits, in bar glasses or wineglasses with appropriate garnishes like lemon and lime slices. Offer alternatives with meals. Most people who don't drink wine will choose water, but some may enjoy coffee or hot or cold tea. If you serve champagne, you can also chill a bottle of sparkling grape juice.

The goal is not to call special attention to guests who don't drink alcohol. Serving all drinks in the same way, for instance, can avoid rude questions about why a guest is not having a cocktail. Also be attentive to seating arrangements. A friend in recovery should not have to spend the evening next to a wine aficionado extolling the virtues of every wine served.

SETTING THE SCENE

Another key ingredient for a successful dinner party is ambience—the mood set by the surroundings. As you prepare, think about how you can best organize your home to make your guests comfortable and complement the meal. Consider your own convenience. As host and perhaps chef and server, you have a lot to do, and your physical surroundings should facilitate your every movement.

The House

A clean and tidy home is the obvious place to start. Even though the party is at night, the exterior should be neat, drives and walkways should be swept and well lighted, and anything that might cause falls, including ice and slush, should be removed. If you live in an apartment, check your hallway for clutter. In inclement weather, think about convenient storage for wet coats, umbrellas, boots, and overshoes that are sure to arrive with guests.

Adequate seating is a must. At very casual dinners, some guests may sit on the floor, but not everyone is comfortable that way, so provide as much seating, including floor pillows, as you can. If you don't have enough chairs, either borrow or rent some or use items like sturdy trunks, low stools, and ottomans that can do double duty as seating and tray tables.

A few more suggestions for setting the scene follow:

REARRANGE FURNITURE AND OTHER ITEMS IF NECESSARY TO FACILITATE CONVERSATION AND FREEDOM OF MOVEMENT. Arrange seats in clusters so that your guests can easily visit. Large pieces of furniture might be shifted if they block easy access to the party areas. Protect valuable items by putting them where they can't be accidentally broken or damaged.

PUT OUT PLENTY OF DRINK COASTERS. Cocktails and other pre-dinner drinks are served with a paper or cloth napkin, but these won't prevent water rings on furniture. If smoking is allowed, be sure to put out ashtrays.

SET DRINK AND BUFFET TABLES APART FROM MAIN GATHERING POINTS AND DOORWAYS. If you use multiple dining tables, be sure there's plenty of passage room for guests to get to their seats and sit without bumping into the person behind them.

BE CONSCIOUS OF FRAGRANCES. Flowers with strong scents, aromatic candles, pungent potpourri, room fresheners, and the like can become stifling in enclosed spaces, set off allergies, and ruin the flavors of the foods you serve.

ADJUST ROOM TEMPERATURES AND LIGHTING. A large group of people will affect the climate of a room, so it's often wise to adjust thermostats before a party (slightly lower than normal heat settings and higher settings for air-conditioned spaces). Adjust as needed during the evening. Lighting should be bright enough for people to see, but not glaring. Table lamps tend to be softer and more flattering than overhead lights, and dimmer switches allow for easy adjustments. Candles provide a warm glow but are inadequate after sundown.

A lighted house always seems to say, "Welcome," so open the curtains or blinds before your guests arrive. You can close them once the party is under way.

SUBDUE THE MUSIC. Recorded classical or contemporary middle-of-the-road instrumental music is usually a safe bet. Be certain the music is just loud enough to be distinct; when turned too low, it becomes an uncomfortable and distracting buzz.

A QUESTION FOR PEGGY

I'm having a buffet supper for twenty, and some of my guests have never been to my condo. My sister says I should be prepared to show off my house, but I'm doing the party by myself, and I just don't have time to clean the upstairs. I'd like to confine the party to my downstairs and backyard.

Except for a housewarming, hosts have no obligation to give house tours, though they may if they want. A host should make it obvious where guests are and are not to go. Before anyone arrives, you can turn off your upstairs hall lights and shut doors to upstairs rooms. Courteous guests know not to open closed doors or enter unlighted areas. If asked for a tour, you (or perhaps your sister) might take a guest on a quick walk through your downstairs. If you see someone wandering into an area where he isn't wanted, divert his attention with some polite chat and gently usher him back to the party area.

The Dinner Table

Table setting is discussed in detail in Chapter 1, page 2: "The Table." The following ideas apply particularly when you entertain at dinner.

TABLE LINENS. Keep tablecloths and place mats uncomplicated. Very frilly or lacy mats, napkins, and table runners and crocheted tablecloths can snag utensils, glass bases, even guests' bracelets and watchbands, causing spills. Plastic tablecloths and mats are fine for casual outdoor dining, but they can detract from the overall appearance of a more formal table. (See also page 163: "The Formal Dinner Party.")

Cloths for dining tables should fall no more than fifteen to eighteen inches below the edge of the table. Cloths for buffet and serving tables may touch the floor. A floor-length cloth on a bar table is a good way to keep bottles, ice chests, and other supplies out of sight. Be sure to equip bar and food stations with plenty of cocktail-sized napkins, paper or cloth.

TABLE DECORATIONS. Flowers and other decorations should be centered on the table and arranged in low containers, so they don't block the view from one side of the table to the other. For the same reason, candelabra are placed with their broad sides facing the ends of the table, and clusters of candlesticks are avoided if they will interfere with guests' line of sight. Candles should be new, unscented, dripless, and burn higher or lower than the eye level of seated diners. Light candles before guests enter the dining area.

Everything on the table should serve the cause of dining, so don't clutter place settings with decorative extras. Guests shouldn't have to forage through table favors, oversized place cards, exotic napkin holders, and other knickknacks to find their plates and utensils. Individual menus are provided only for the most formal dinners.

Flowers are pretty on buffet tables, if there's room. Arranging buffet food at different height levels, while intended to showcase the food, can actually impede self-service and sometimes put a dish literally beyond a guest's reach.

BUFFET TABLES. The placement of dinner plates indicates the starting point of a buffet table. On a large or round table, putting plates in the center gives no clear place to begin and also forces guests to reach over the food. Although silverware and napkins may be arranged next to the plates, placing utensils at the end of the buffet frees guests from carrying too many items as they serve themselves.

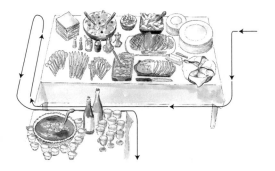

Traffic pattern around a buffet table: A table against a wall.

You can also provide dinner trays—set with utensils and napkins—at the end of the serving table. For a seated semi-buffet, dining tables are set with everything except plates.

The arrangement of the food on a buffet is up to you, though gravies and sauces are placed beside the dishes they accompany and breads are often available at the end of the line. (If bread and rolls are placed on the plate first, they can become soggy with sauces, meat juices, and dressings.)

When serving drinks buffet-style, it's usually

more convenient to use a separate table. Guests can take their filled plates to the table or wherever they are sitting and then return to the drink table. Expecting guests to juggle a full plate, utensils, and napkin while pouring a beverage is an open invitation to accidents.

Traffic pattern around a buffet table:
A table in the center of a room.

LET THE PARTY BEGIN

A host or hosts should be ready on the dot to answer the door, greet guests, and take coats. After a gracious greeting, you'll want to offer each new arrival something to drink. But don't abandon a guest at the door in order to get him a cocktail. Usher guests to the party area, make introductions as necessary, and then get the drink or direct the guest to the drink table.

If separate groups of guests arrive at the same time, welcome everyone inside first, then make introductions. (When you're a guest, don't stop to chat at the door, especially if there are other guests behind you.) A single host may have to do some fancy footwork when guests come in rapid-fire order, so it's pragmatic to ask one or two good friends to help with introductions and beverages. Couples and co-hosts can share greeting responsibilities.

Once everyone has arrived, a host should mix and mingle while attending to these essential courtesies:

ENCOURAGE CONVERSATION. When introducing guests for the first time, bring up subjects they may have in common. If you see someone on his own or trapped in a conversation, politely go to the rescue.

PASS HORS D'OEUVRES AND OFFER TO REPLENISH DRINKS. Refill bowls of munchies before the last olive or pretzel disappears.

PICK UP EMPTY, ABANDONED DRINK GLASSES. Dump out and wipe ashtrays. In other words, police the party area, but don't be obsessive.

CHECK PERIODICALLY ON BAR SUPPLIES AND NAPKINS. Refill ice buckets as needed.

TAKE QUICK PEEKS IN BATH AND POWDER ROOMS TO SEE THAT EVERYTHING IS IN ORDER. Replace soiled or wet hand towels.

Dinner Is Served

When the group is small, the host simply announces that dinner is served. With larger numbers, the host or hosts approach conversation groups and invite them into the dining area. Try to spot a few good friends who will begin the movement; most people will follow. Ringing a bell or sounding a gong is an antiquated custom but might be fun if it fits with the theme of the evening, such as a Victorian dinner.

Seating shouldn't be a problem if you've planned in advance. Place cards are easiest with a larger group—eight or more at the table—and when multiple tables are used. Otherwise, guests will look to the host for guidance.

THE ETIQUETTE OF COCKTAIL GLASSES AND WINEGLASSES

If you're holding a partly consumed cocktail when dinner is announced, you can take it to the table and finish it before the meal begins. Or you can leave your glass on a side table, atop a coaster or glass-topped surface. Just don't take an empty drink glass to the table. Do the same with a wineglass. A host should not expect guests to use the same glasses for pre-dinner and dinner wines.

Specialty beers are increasingly popular as an aperitif and are usually served in a tumbler or Pilsner glass. Sometimes a bottle and empty glass are provided so the guest can pour for himself, but beer and soda are served in cans or bottles only at the most casual affairs.

At the dinner table, don't turn wineglasses upside down to indicate you don't want wine. Instead, you should simply say, "No, thank you," when wine is offered. Or put your hand over the glass (above, not on, the rim) to signal a server to pass you by. An experienced server will then remove the glass.

CONVIVIAL SEATING. Man-woman-man-woman seating is no longer a rule. Gender-specific seating really doesn't fit an age when men and women frequently attend events by themselves or with same-sex partners. Aim instead to seat guests between people with whom they're likely to be congenial. It's still a good idea to separate married couples and close friends simply because they are likely to converse too much with each other or discuss domestic subjects that others cannot join in. Think about your guests' personalities. If you seat a shy person next to a very talkative one, the shy guest may spend the entire meal in enforced silence.

HONORED GUESTS. A female guest of honor sits to the immediate right of the host, a male honor guest to the immediate right of the hostess. If there is one host or hostess, the honor guest may be seated next to the host/hostess or at the opposite end of the table. But these guidelines are flexible.

A SPECIAL CONSIDERATION. If you can, seat left-handed guests at the left end of each side of the table, where they are less likely to bump elbows with right-handed neighbors.

WHEN TO START EATING. Hosts traditionally

take the first bite of food to signal guests to begin eating. Some hosts observe rituals such as saying a blessing. But when you're serving, you may want to tell your guests to begin eating before you, so their food won't go cold; it's fine for guests to start eating before the host does if he encourages them to do so. At a buffet, guests normally begin eating when they sit down.

Hosts should be conscious of the dinner conversation, guiding it if necessary. Don't be panicked by natural lulls; people tend to stop talking when a course is served and they begin to eat. Then the chatter picks up. Be alert to uncomfortable situations. When one person is dominating the table talk, you can direct questions to those who aren't holding sway. If an issue is raised that you know is troubling for some guests, bring up an entirely new subject. A considerate host is always gracious . . . and sometimes a little firm.

After Dessert

Coffee and cordials are served either at the table or in the living room. Though coffee traditionally follows a meal, it's fine to serve coffee with dessert if your guests prefer. A host is not obligated to offer after-dinner drinks, and today's hosts might pass up this finishing touch if guests are driving home.

CLEARING THE TABLE

Places are cleared between courses, including the utensils used for that course and empty wineglasses if you will be serving another wine. Even at casual dinners, plates shouldn't be stacked or scraped at the table. Remove one or two plates at a time. Don't ask people to pass plates, utensils, or glasses to you unless the items are beyond your reach.

Bread plates and butter knives are left on the table until the dessert course. Salad plates are not taken away until the diner is finished. If someone has used the wrong knife or fork for a course, don't ask her to hold on to it. Replace the utensil (which may necessitate a quick wash and dry in the kitchen).

The process of clearing may sound time-consuming, but actually it goes quickly and is a lot easier and safer than balancing stacks of china and handfuls of silverware. It goes even faster if two people are clearing, so when you don't have servers, arrange in advance for a friend to help. You'll be too busy serving the next course to wash dishes or load the dishwasher, so plan for a place in the kitchen where dirty plates and dinnerware can be placed.

Fresh fruit and/or cheese might be served after dessert, and hosts may put out after-dinner mints and nuts. (At a formal dinner, bowls of mints and nuts can be placed on the table as decorative items, then offered at the end of the dinner.) However, when the meal is over, hosts aren't expected to continue providing food. Assuming that the meal has been sufficient, the after-dinner hour is your reward—a time to relax with your guests and enjoy the pleasant afterglow of your hard work.

Conversation is the most popular after-dinner activity, but guests may enjoy listening to music, dancing, or playing games such as Trivial Pursuit, Pictionary, and charades. Which activity to choose depends on the mood of the evening, and no one should be goaded into participating.

Saying Farewell

All good things must end, and well-mannered guests will know when to depart. Hosts should be on hand to say farewell and show their guests to the door.

Don't begin cleaning up or washing dishes until your guests have gone (unless someone has seriously overstayed his welcome and more subtle hints have failed). In general, if a guest offers to help you clean up, respond with a pleasantly firm, "Oh, this is your night out. We're not doing dishes now. Thanks for offering, though." The exception is if guests are close friends or family members and it's customary that you all pitch in when dining at each other's homes. If guests brought food, you may want to return their serving dishes washed and dried. If you borrowed items for the party, it's probably best to return them the next day or within a few days.

If you've hired servers or caterers, you must see that they are dismissed with your thanks (and payment if that is the arrangement). A good host doesn't delay an employee's departure beyond an agreed-on time. If you want a worker or workers to stay throughout the party, be sure that this is clear when you contract for services.

A host's last duty is to see that guests depart safely and soberly. Do not under any circumstances allow an inebriated guest to drive. Another guest might take the person home. You might call for a cab; pay for it if you must. In the worst case, you may have to put your guest to bed for the night. Don't worry about embarrassing a guest who has overindulged. What matters is that the person is alive the next day to regret his or her behavior.

A DOZEN DINNER GUEST DO'S AND DON'TS

Good guest manners begin the moment you receive a dinner invitation and continue beyond the end of the evening.

Do respond to an RSVP as quickly as possible. If the invitation includes "and Guest," tell the host whether you plan to bring someone—even when you don't yet know whom. Call the host with the name of your guest as soon as you can.

Don't bring a guest unless invited to do so. Regardless of the circumstances, don't ask a host if you can bring a guest. Parents must remember that if children are not included in the invitation, they aren't invited.

Do arrive on time. Five or ten minutes after the start time is okay. No guest should show up early. If the invitation says "around six," this means between six o'clock and six-fifteen. If you're going to be more than fifteen minutes late, call, explain quickly, and give the host an estimated arrival time. A host should not be expected to delay a meal longer than fifteen minutes for a latecomer.

Do bring a gift if appropriate. It's nice to present a host or hostess with a token of appreciation—a bottle of wine (but don't expect it to be served), candy, or gift soaps. If you send flowers, call the host in advance to check on the party color scheme, or, better yet, send an arrangement on the day after the party, with a nice note. If you take flowers to the party, be sure they're in a vase. (A busy host doesn't have time to search for a container and arrange your flowers.) Don't bring food unless specifically requested. People who dine frequently with one another are not expected to bring gifts on every occasion.

Don't gather in the kitchen unless the host asks you to. Some people love to cook with an audience; others really can't concentrate. You can offer to help a host who is cooking, but don't insist if she or he turns you down.

Don't change place cards or ask to sit in a special place at a seated dinner. Hosts put a good deal of thought into seating arrangements, and a polite guest doesn't try to out-think them. It's rude to manipulate seating in any way.

Do compliment the food graciously. Just be realistic. (The soufflé may be marvelous, but don't say that it's the best you ever tasted unless you mean it.)

You're commenting on the food, so avoid back-handed compliments like "I never guessed you could cook this well." If you know the host didn't cook, don't mention it unless he or she does. The host will convey your compliments to a cook or caterer.

Don't be a double dipper. One chip, cracker, shrimp, veggie, or fruit tidbit is for one dip, and only one, in the bowl. Double dipping is unsanitary and inconsiderate of the hosts, who will have to toss out a dip when they catch a double dipper.

Do be on your best behavior. Unless asked by the host, don't open closed doors, cabinets, drawers, and medicine chests. Tidy the bathroom after use. (Hang guest towels neatly on the rack, but don't refold them.) If you don't see ashtrays, go outside to smoke if you must. Don't inquire about the cost of anything.

Don't let your cell phone interrupt. Turn ringers and beepers off. If you must call, go to a secluded spot. If you need to use your host's phone, ask for permission. If you expect to receive a call during the party, ask the hosts before giving their number to anyone. Don't answer a host's phone unless he or she requests you to.

Don't be the last to leave. Unless a host specifically asks you to stay, it's best to make your departure when other guests begin to leave. In general, guests are expected to stay for at least an hour after dinner. If you must leave early, inform the host before the party or when you arrive.

Do thank your hosts—all of them—when you leave. You may want to follow up with a thank-you note, but personal notes are expected only for formal dinner parties. Otherwise, call the host within a day or two or send an e-mail if that's the best way to reach the person. If there were multiple hosts, you might call everyone or just the one or two you know best.

Above all, never abuse a host's trust. When a guest accepts an invitation, he or she enters into a kind of unwritten social contract to act responsibly. Excessive drinking, drug use, aggressive behavior, crude language—these behaviors violate the fundamentals of decency. Hosts commit themselves to make the occasion pleasant and safe. Guests should do no less.

THE FORMAL DINNER PARTY

There's formal, and then there's FORMAL. At the highest end of the formality scale are official dinners hosted by or for high-ranking public officials and diplomats. These events are governed by strict protocol, and guests are informed of (and often instructed in) the rules by protocol officers.

For most people, a formal dinner is one at which they are seated at a dining table and the entire meal is served by someone other than themselves. A very formal evening for more than six or eight is difficult for a host who handles cooking and service. If you don't have household employees, then hiring servers for the night will enable you to prepare a delicious meal and then enjoy it with your guests.

People today tend to regard at-home formal dining as an opportunity to dress up, set a beautiful table, use their very best manners, and enjoy lively conversation over an excellent meal. There are, however, some fine points of etiquette for very formal meals, and many of these manners apply equally well to more casual dining.

➤ A housekeeper, butler, other domestic employee, or a willing family member may open the door to guests, take their coats, and show them to the party area where they are immediately greeted by the hosts. The hosts should be present to greet and mingle during the traditional pre-dinner "cocktail hour," which may be shorter than an hour but rarely longer.

➤ If place cards are used, the host or hostess enters the dining room after all the guests. Otherwise, the host or hostess leads the way and indicates where guests are to sit.

➤ Women sit down as soon as they find their places; men stand at their places until the hostess is seated or the host signals them to be seated. In the traditional man-woman-man-woman order, each man customarily holds the chair of the woman on his right, but women today often seat themselves if they wish. Guests of honor sit to the right of the hostess and host; otherwise, hosts determine the seating order.

➤ The formal table is laid with a *white* cloth of damask, linen, or lace, which falls no more than eighteen inches below the edge of the table. Matching white napkins are a generous size: approximately twenty-four inches square. Damask cloths are laid over a felt pad or white blanket folded to fit the table; linen and lace cloths are placed directly on the table surface. To be truly formal, candles in the dining room are white.

➢ Plates are served from the diner's left side but removed from the right. No serving dishes or platters are put on the table, and meat is not carved at the table. Plates (warmed for hot courses) are filled in the kitchen or at a side table and placed before each diner. Salt and pepper containers are placed on the table, but vegetables, breads, and condiments are passed by the server; diners take adequate portions, and the serving dishes are returned to the kitchen or sideboard. (When there is more than one server, one will normally set the plates with the main item before each diner, and another server will follow, offering vegetables, bread, etc.) All plates are removed between courses, as are the utensils used for that course—but only when *all* diners have finished with the course.

A charger, or service plate, is a large plate (usually twelve inches in diameter) that is put on the table with the place setting and not removed until the main course is served. (See Chapter 1, page 5: "Service plate.")

➢ Wine is served from the right before each

FINGER BOWL FINESSE

Finger bowls are for cleaning fingers and reducing stains on napkins (not for drinking or rinsing food or utensils). And quite useful amenities they are, especially if you have something greasy or sticky on your digits. There's really nothing mysterious about finger bowls.

Most often seen at a formal dinner, a finger bowl is a smallish glass bowl containing cool or lukewarm water and sometimes a small fresh flower. The bowl is usually brought in on the dessert plate just before dessert arrives. You dip only your fingers—one hand at a time—into the water, rub or swish gently, shake off excess water with equal caution, and then use your dinner napkin to dry your fingers. The whole thing is done in a matter of seconds. When finished, you lift the finger bowl and the little doily it was placed on and move them to the upper left of your place setting.

You might also encounter a finger bowl with a thin slice of lemon instead of a flower after a more informal, hands-on meal, such as one with lobster. The lemon helps to cut the grease. After you've dipped your fingers, as above, either a server will remove the bowl or you can move it to the side of your place setting.

course and replenished as needed. The wineglasses at each place indicate the number of different wines to be served. Water glasses are refilled throughout the evening. Coffee cups and saucers are usually not included in the original place setting, but they may be if a guest prefers coffee or tea with his meal.

➢ The salad course generally follows the main course, but if salad accompanies the entrée, it is served on a separate plate. The salad is usually dressed, either in the kitchen or at a side table, just before it is served.

➢ Dessert forks and spoons may be set on the table with the original place setting (positioned horizontally above the plate) or brought to the table with the dessert course.

➢ The server may sweep the table between courses, using a tightly folded napkin to brush crumbs into a plate or a silent butler held just below the table edge. This is done unobtrusively so that conversation isn't interrupted. The server will add or replace knives, forks, and spoons as needed.

➢ Coffee and tea may be served at the table or when the guests retire to the living room. The host or hostess may pour, or the hot coffee can be brought to each guest from the kitchen or a serving table. Since tastes vary, put sugar bowls and creamers (plus a bowl of sugar substitute packets) on the table or on a tray passed to guests. Coffee spoons are placed on the saucer. After-dinner cordials and fortified wines like port are served with the coffee course.

LUNCH, BRUNCH, AND OTHER DINING OCCASIONS

Though considerably refined across 30,000 years of civilization, the impulse to share one's table with friends and strangers alike seems basic to all cultures. The evening dinner party is particularly suited to today's busy schedules, but whatever the time of day and degree of informality, entertaining good company at a meal is hospitality at its best.

Luncheons

When convenient, the lunch hour can be the perfect time to gather friends and colleagues and perhaps conduct a little business. Though luncheons are often held at restaurants and clubs, an at-home lunch is a very nice way to host a club or committee meeting, entertain business associates, and honor out-of-town visitors and special guests.

Traditional lunch parties, including bridge and bridal luncheons, remain popular but are often scheduled on weekends so that guests won't have to worry about getting back to work.

Luncheon food is normally lighter than dinner fare: a starter or salad course and an entrée, a salad or soup and sandwich, or a bountiful luncheon salad—plus dessert and coffee. Because many people prefer not to drink alcohol in the middle of the day, it has become less common to offer cocktails, but guests might enjoy a glass of sherry or a nonalcoholic drink. Wine may accompany the meal, but water, iced tea, and fruit drinks are the mainstays of luncheon beverages.

Whether a lunch is seated or buffet, the etiquette varies little from the basics of dinner parties. The main difference is that food and service are often streamlined. During business hours, lunch may last for no more than an hour, so the meal begins soon after guests arrive and serving tends to be informal. With careful planning, the occasion will not seem rushed. Hosts have to be attentive to the time constraints of their guests, just as guests should not be tempted to linger when the host must return to his or her job.

Breakfast

A breakfast party is a more elaborate version of the everyday morning meal. Breakfasts can begin as early as 8:30 or as late as 10:00 am and often precede an occasion such as a graduation ceremony, a morning wedding, a noontime sports event, or a business meeting. (Traditionally, breakfast buffets are served after midnight at balls and formal dances, but these are catered at the event site.)

The menu is based on the classic eggs-bacon-toast formula. Dishes such as eggs Benedict, omelets, ham and biscuits, French toast, Belgian waffles, and sweet pastries are typical, though hosts should also provide alternatives like fresh and stewed fruits and low-cholesterol quick breads for health-conscious guests. A variety of juices as well as coffee and tea are served; alcoholic drinks are not. Breakfast is usually a buffet and can be served in the kitchen if you have a large enough space.

Brunch

Brunch, combining the virtues of a late breakfast and an early lunch, seems made for leisurely weekend get-togethers. Brunches might also be associated with other social activities—a gathering for out-of-town guests on the day after a wedding or graduation, for example.

Typically, brunches begin around 11:00 am or noon. A brunch can be a seated affair, but informal buffets are more popular, and even relatively formal brunches have a casual mood. Menus typically blend traditional breakfast and lunch fare: creamed chicken on waffles, sausage or ham rolls, mushroom quiches, frittata, seafood casserole, fruit compote, green salads. Foods tend to be light and often feature fresh fruits and vegetables in season.

Bloody Marys, with or without alcohol, and mimosas (champagne and orange juice) are often served, as are lighter white and blush wines. But have plenty of nonalcoholic beverages available. Alcohol-free fruit punches go well with brunch food and add a colorful touch to the buffet.

Late Suppers

When people don't have the time or appetite for a meal before a night at the theater, a concert, or a sports event, a late supper is a good way to draw the evening to its end. When you host an intimate group of friends, the atmosphere is relaxed and convivial. The supper menu is lighter and less extensive than a full dinner. Choose foods you can prepare in advance and assemble quickly or whip up at the last minute, like omelets. If you include dessert, serve something refreshing—a fruit ice, for example. (Quality chocolates and mints or cookies served with coffee can easily substitute for a dessert course.) Light wine is a pleasant accompaniment, depending on the lateness of the hour, but guests may prefer water, coffee, or another nonalcoholic beverage. Service tends to be informal—from a buffet or on dinner trays—no matter how simple or elegant the meal.

A TIDY ENDING FOR OUTSIDE OCCASIONS

At picnics, tailgate parties, and other events at outside locations, cleanup is an absolute. Use waste containers available at the site or bring your own. Don't leave any food behind; your leftovers will attract animals. Pick up and dispose of every bit of litter, including cigarette butts, drink cans, and pull-tabs. Outdoor cooking—if allowed—is a fire hazard, so take a fire extinguisher. Be sure that all fires, including those in grills, are completely out before leaving the site; douse coals with water and rake ashes for any smoldering embers. Someone must clean up the mess, and the ultimate responsibility falls on the host. Even if you miss the kick-off or first inning, do the right thing and leave the area clean and safe for the people who use it next.

Picnics and Barbecues

Day or night, picnics and barbecues seem to exemplify the American style of home entertaining. The informal nature of the typical backyard gathering makes it a popular last-minute activity. But even the most casual event needs organization, so plan ahead when you can. By issuing invitations a few days to a week before the party, you have a better chance of assuring that people can attend.

Picnic and barbecue menus are virtually limitless. If others bring food, you'll want to coordinate so that you don't wind up with too much of the same thing. (See "Potluck Suppers," below.) Be very conscious of food safety: Keep foods at the correct temperatures and don't leave foods out for longer than an hour—a half hour in warm weather. (For information about food storage and handling, with links to other sources, search at www.foodsafety.gov, a service of the U.S. government.)

BYOB, or "bring your own bottle," on an invitation indicates that guests are expected to supply their beverages. Usually, this means alcoholic drinks, and the hosts provide basics—sodas, bottled water, and perhaps tea and fruit juice—as well as ice and drink glasses.

An etiquette note: Consider neighbors when

grilling or barbecuing—especially if you live in close quarters. If outdoor cooking is permitted, be sure the cooking area is well ventilated so that smoke and odors don't collect in hallways or blow into a neighbor's windows.

Potluck Suppers

Potluck suppers are a fun way for family and friends to share their bounty in a casual and inexpensive way. Basically, a potluck (or covered dish) supper is organized by one or several people or a group, and everyone who comes contributes something to the meal. Be clear when issuing a potluck invitation. "Potluck" means that all guests share the food. The notation BYOF literally means "bring *your own* food," and guests will show up with food for themselves, not dishes to be shared.

Organization is important so that the potluck menu will be varied. Participants might be given a choice of foods within categories (salads, vegetables, breads, casseroles, desserts). To assure a balanced spread, the organizers should know what participants plan to bring. Participants are also informed how many people will attend so they can prepare adequate quantities.

Sometimes organizers provide an entrée such as fried chicken or burgers and hot dogs or a dessert like homemade ice cream. Those who don't cook can bring packaged items like buns and chips or paper plates and napkins, coolers and ice, or bags of charcoal. The organizers may provide drinks, but if alcoholic beverages are included, participants often bring their own.

Progressive Dinners

The progressive dinner, a popular nineteenth-century entertainment that has undergone a revival with the growth of cooking and gourmet clubs, is similar to a potluck in that several participants provide the food. The difference is that each course is prepared by a different cook. Traditionally, guests go from house to house, and the number of homes visited depends on the number of courses served. Today's progressive party might be held at one location, though different cooks prepare and serve each course.

The dinner might be organized by the hosts or by a group such as a food or wine club or it might be held to celebrate a holiday. Menus are carefully planned and coordinated, and the people who aren't cooking are considered guests for the occasion, though they may assist with serving. Progressive dinners can range from very casual to very formal. When held at several homes, each host usually decides the format (seated, buffet, semi-buffet) for his or her course.

Groups that regularly hold progressive dinners may not be too concerned about costs because expenses tend to even out as group members rotate cooking assignments. But hosts of a one-time progressive dinner should address food and beverage costs as a first step, so one host doesn't bear an unreasonable share.

Wine-tasting Dinners

Friends who share an interest in wines get together for a multi-course dinner (or sometimes lunch) in order to enjoy different wine varieties served with appropriate foods. Wine-tasting dinners might have a single host but are often staged by groups of wine lovers on a fairly regular basis. One person usually selects the wines to be served. A sparkling wine is often tasted first, followed by a selection of whites and reds during dinner and a sweet dessert wine to finish.

Before each wine is tasted, the person who chose it will talk a little about the wine and the reasons for his or her choice. A guest shouldn't take a sip before the spiel is finished. Nor should anyone ask for a wine that isn't being served.

Chapter Four

HOSTS AND HOUSEGUESTS

Perhaps you've invited your sister and brother-in-law, who live in another town, to be your guests over Labor Day weekend. Or you opened an e-mail from a friend to find he will be passing through your city and wonders if you know of any good hotels—and you reply that he's welcome to stay in your guest room. Whether by design or accident, you've taken on the role of host and all its attendant duties.

Having friends or relatives stay overnight or for the weekend gives you the opportunity to relax, have more time to talk, plan activities you all enjoy, and share several meals together. But hosts and guests alike have a rather delicate balancing act to perform. The former's most important task is making his guests feel at home. The latter's duty is to behave differently than he would at his own. That means refraining from keeping to his own schedule, helping himself to food in the fridge without permission, taking control of the remote, and so forth. Also, behaviors that might not be noticed over the course of an evening can begin to grate after two or three days—exactly the opposite of what everyone wants.

This chapter begins with the responsibilities of hosts, with guidelines for everything from preparing for your houseguests to welcoming them and bidding them adieu, then switches to pointers for the guests.

FIRST MOVES

Hosting can involve inviting a person for one night or a group for a long weekend (an occasion still referred to as a house party in some parts of the United States), or any variation thereof. Begin by laying out the particulars as clearly as possible: When will the guests arrive? When will they be leaving? A phone call followed with a note or e-mail will prevent confusion over dates and times. Also let guests know whether you have anything planned for their stay, and on which days—a dinner at a high-end restaurant (which means dressing up a bit) or any other event for which they may have to bring something.

If your guests are coming by car, make sure they know the way—and that means not limiting your directions to a phone call. To ensure that guests understand and have a take-along copy, write the directions down and send or e-mail them in advance. If guests will be arriving by train or plane, discuss the options for getting to your house—being picked up by you or a car service, for example, or taking a taxi or public transportation.

Welcoming Houseguests

Once your guests arrive, show them to their room or sleeping area and the bath they will use. Then give them a chance to tidy up and unpack. If they're unfamiliar with your home, conduct a quick tour whenever they're ready: the bathroom, cabinets for towels and other items, light switches, the telephone, and kitchen appliances. Show them how to adjust the air conditioner or heater, if necessary. Then tell them to help themselves to snacks or beverages from the fridge during their stay, noting any foods that are off-limits: "Please help yourself to anything you see except the blueberries—they're for the pancakes tomorrow morning."

No Guest Room?

If you live in a one-bedroom apartment or a house with no guest room, don't think you can't play host. A sofa bed, futon, or air bed can be set up in the living room or den, or children could be doubled up to vacate a room if the visit isn't lengthy. (In the latter case, arrange the toys neatly, remove some clothes from the closet, clear enough drawer space for the guest's needs, and make sure the room is sparkling clean.)

The important thing is to give your guests advance warning that they won't have a separate room or that they'll have to share a room. While some guests may be perfectly fine having to sleep on a sofa or air bed in the den, others may choose not to come if they have to make do with makeshift or shared quarters. Even then, it's not a good idea to move out of your own room so you can give it to your guests, since they would almost certainly feel they were imposing.

CHECKLIST FOR HOSTS

Here's a checklist of the items and comforts you should attend to, plus a few optional ones that will add a nice touch.

IN THE GUEST ROOM OR SLEEPING AREA . . .

➢ Bed, sofa bed, futon, or air bed made up with clean sheets and pillowcases

➤ Extra blanket at the foot of the bed

➤ A good reading light at each bed

➤ Clock radio

➤ Box of tissues on the nightstand

➤ Wastebasket

➤ Coat hangers in the closet

➤ Luggage rack, if you own one

IN THE BATHROOM . . .

➤ Fresh bath towels, face towels, washcloths, bath mat

➤ Fresh cakes of soap

➤ Glasses for drinking and brushing teeth

➤ New roll of toilet paper in the dispenser and an unopened one in the cabinet

➤ Box of tissues

NICE TOUCHES . . .

➤ Vase of flowers

➤ Calendar

➢ Reading matter (magazines, short books)

➢ Two pillows for each guest—one medium-firm and one soft

➢ Wooden coat hangers with bars or pressure clips for trousers; plastic hangers for dresses

➢ Clothes brush, lint roller, and pincushion stuck with both safety pins and straight pins

➢ Shampoo, bath oil, bath powder, and hand lotion on the washstand

➢ New toothbrush, just in case the guest has forgotten her own

➢ Headache and stomachache medicines in the guest bathroom medicine cabinet

Schedules and Routines

Share your routines with the guests: "Sunday is our morning to sleep in—if you get up first, the bread and English muffins are in the bread drawer and the coffeemaker will be all ready to go—just push the start button." Also give them a heads-up on any absences you foresee: "I have to go to a meeting Monday morning, so I'm leaving you on your own. I should be back around eleven o'clock."

If your guests are visiting during weekdays, it's

important that you share your normal schedule with them so that they can plan their time accordingly. ("Mom and Dad, the girls leave for school at seven-thirty, so we're up and running at about six forty-five. I wanted to warn you because that's when they take over the bathroom.") This is a gentle way to familiarize your visitors with the way things are done in your household and help them to fit right in. If they know that after arriving home from work you need a ten-minute break and a clothes change, your guests will be less likely to greet you at the door expecting to chat about what everyone's been doing.

This doesn't mean expecting your visitors to do everything your way; they're your guests, and their happiness and comfort are as important as yours. Yes, your routine will be disrupted, but the more forthcoming you can be about what happens when—and why—the more pleasurable the visit will be for everyone.

Easing Your Way

You can save yourself a lot of trouble by preparing whatever you can in advance—mainly meals. Any number of cookbooks feature make-ahead dishes of every sort, and one with exceptionally good recipes can become a host's best friend. Even if you can't prepare all the meals ahead of time, plan your menus and stock your kitchen with whatever ingredients you'll need; otherwise, you'll have to spend time shopping after your guests have arrived.

The one meal that you can't easily organize in advance is breakfast. Because one of the joys of a weekend away from home is being able to sleep late, a good host doesn't awaken guests unless they've asked to be. Unless you've told your guests to help themselves to breakfast, make coffee and put out eggs, fruit, cereals, or other breakfast foods before they rise. It's okay to go ahead and eat — but if you do, be there to help guests as they arrive.

When good friends are visiting, don't be afraid to ask them to pitch in: "Belinda, would you mind reading the children a bedtime story while I get dinner ready?" Or "Tom, would you please watch the grill for a few minutes?" And don't refuse their offers. Most guests sincerely want to help and might feel uncomfortable if they're consistently rebuffed.

When the Kids Come

The children of houseguests may either utterly charm everyone present or run around like little hellions. But if the host has children of roughly the same age, the battle is half won: The kids can often be left to themselves and can also play with neighborhood children. Even if the host has no

A QUESTION FOR PEGGY

My son and his girlfriend are students at a nearby college, and we've invited them to spend their Thanksgiving break with us. The problem is, they've been living together for six months, an arrangement that we're not happy about. How should we handle the situation?

Parents have a right to insist that their standards be observed in their own home, and you should make that clear to your son. If he says, "Well, then we won't be able to come," you have to decide whether your relationship and continued communication with him is more important than upholding your standards. (This is an individual matter of conscience, not one of etiquette.) Still, you can stand your ground. If you and your son understand each other and have a good relationship to begin with, he's more likely to accept the rules you establish than to put you in a difficult position. Just be sure to let your feelings be known from the very beginning—not when he and his girlfriend are carrying their bags up the stairs.

children, she might arrange a playdate for her visitors and other kids in her neighborhood.

Treating any child who is present with tolerance and respect—not as a pint-sized interloper who should be seen but not heard—will make everyone's stay that much easier. Parents obviously shouldn't shirk their duties, no matter how much they're looking forward to a relaxing visit. It's their responsibility—and theirs alone—to keep their children in line, clean up after them, and get them to bed at their regular hour.

When Guests Depart

Under normal circumstances, do what you can to make your guests' departure as easy as possible—enlisting your teenager to carry their bags to the car or asking them whether they double-checked to make sure they left nothing behind. Even if guests must get up at 4:00 am to catch a plane and you choose to stay in bed, you can help with their departure plans ahead of time—say, arranging for a taxi.

Naturally, you'll tell guests how much you enjoyed their stay and that you hope they'll come again. A polite host not only sees his guests to the door but also stands on the porch until they're out of sight, waving the occasional good-bye. Were he to disappear from view, he could leave the impression he's eager to get back to his routine.

(He probably is, but in the spirit of good manners he would never admit it.)

THE GUEST WHO STAYS TOO LONG

The problem of guests overstaying their welcome is so universal that it has given rise to proverbs for centuries. Most of us know of the one that equates houseguests with fish: Both "start to stink in three days." But a Portuguese proverb says it more subtly: "Visits always give pleasure—if not the coming, then the going."

So what is a good host to do? Not much besides dropping a few hints, and then remembering the houseguest's thoughtlessness before deciding whether to invite her again.

➤ Let her know you've enjoyed her visit but that it's important that you return to your regular schedule.

➤ Don't feel obligated to keep entertaining her.

➤ If applicable, mention a specific time and event: "Dan is coming home on Friday, so I'm afraid we're going to need his room back."

Note: If the guest has to stay longer because of airline cancellations or other unavoidable problems, be as helpful as you can. The situation is probably as difficult for her as it is for you.

Recording Visits

A tradition that abides is a guest book for guests to sign, often with a comment on their stay: "Great company, great conversation, great food! Thanks for a weekend we'll always remember." Good stationery stores sell books for the purpose, so you can find one that fits your style, from ultracasual to formal.

Keeping a second record is purely practical. In a notebook, the host can list foods that were served so that she doesn't offer the same dishes when the guests return; any foods that guests particularly liked or disliked or are allergic to; and the activities and events that occurred. For example, if the Braders last visited you two years ago and were taken to the old mill and the town museum, a note to this effect is a reminder to make other plans the next time around.

TWELVE HOST GIFT IDEAS

Houseguests are expected to give a gift to the host(s). For an overnight stay, something on the order of a bottle of good wine is sufficient. A longer stay requires an item that's a little more expensive. If the hosts have young children, it's also nice to present a small token gift to each one.

You can take a gift with you and present it as soon as you arrive or could buy one during your stay. (You might get a good idea of what the host wants or needs after a day or two.) A third option is to send a gift as soon as possible after you leave.

An important consideration: Decorative items with simple designs and neutral colors are safer choices than those with bright colors and busy patterns. Everyone will appreciate an unadorned silver-plate picture frame, while a frame adorned with birds, hearts, or stars may not be to the recipient's taste.

Other gift ideas:

➤ New best-selling book you know will interest the host

➤ Hand towels for the powder room or beach towels for sunning

➤ Packages of cocktail napkins, perhaps with the host's monogram

➤ Desk calendar for the coming year (appropriate in late fall or winter)

➤ Bottle of liqueur or cognac you know the host is fond of

➢ Sturdy canvas tote bag (preferably without a logo)

➢ For a keen cook, two or three unusual kitchen utensils, such as a pasta lifter or egg separator

➢ For a golfer, a dozen golf balls

➢ Set of nicely packaged herbs and spices or a selection of peppercorns (black, white, red, green)

➢ Picture frame, with a picture taken during your visit sent later

➢ Candles and informal candlesticks

➢ Houseplant in a permanent, simple-yet-decorative pot

DO'S AND DON'TS FOR HOUSEGUESTS

There's more to being a good houseguest than just being nice and doing your part to help out. Here are some important things to consider when you plan to stay over at someone's home:

Do bring your own toiletries. Don't count on your host having stocked the guest bathroom cabinet with everything you might need.

Do offer to help. Any time you see a chance to

help the host, do offer—but be specific. "I'll peel the carrots"; "It's my turn to clear the table"; or "Let me take those packages in." At the same time, don't overdo it. Prowling about the kitchen just waiting for an opportunity to pitch in can be distracting to the cook.

Do be adaptable. Be ready for anything—or for nothing. If your host has planned a swim in the lake and you're not a swimmer, be enthusiastic nonetheless: "I can't swim, but I'll love sitting on the bank and watching." Conversely, if your host has nothing planned and you're at a loss for what to do, settle in with a good book or take walks, now and then letting the host know what a nice, relaxing time you're having.

Do tidy up after yourself. Unless the host has household help and instructs you not to, straighten up your room and make the bed (see page 197: "How to Leave the Bed"). Keep your bathroom immaculate, especially if you're sharing it with other people. Don't leave a ring in the tub, a rim of shaving cream in the basin, hair on any object or surface, or dirt on the soap. If no sponge is handy, either ask for one or use a paper towel or tissues to wipe up.

Do appear to enjoy yourself. Even if you aren't having the best time, act as if you couldn't be more pleased. In this case, pretending isn't really deceitful: It's courteous, considering that your host's knowledge of your unhappiness could ruin the weekend.

Do ensure your host has some time alone. Usually, both guest and host need some "breathing room" away from each other, and it's often easier for the guest to suggest a way to make it happen. "Ed, I've taken up walking for an hour every day and thought I'd do it now unless there's something you've got scheduled." This gives him the opportunity to say, "Now's a fine time. I have some paperwork to do, so I'll tackle it while you're out."

Do host your hosts. If your stay is for three days or more, tell your hosts before you arrive that you would like to take them out to dinner one evening. Then also handle the reservations and pick up all expenses—not only the meal but also tips, cab fares, and so forth. A dinner isn't the only way to express your gratitude, of course; one alternative is to take your hosts to a movie and out for drinks or supper afterward.

Do have a supply of portable snacks if you've

brought your children. Granola bars, bottled juices, and the like will stave off the kids' hunger pangs until mealtime. It's probable that the host will offer to forage around for food to keep the little ones happy, but a parent can also prepare a snack from the food in the refrigerator if the host has given blanket permission to "help yourselves."

Do treat any household help courteously. If during your visit any household employees come on duty, greet them as you would anyone else and thank them if they aid you in any way. Don't tip an employee unless she volunteers to run an errand or perform any other special service—and even then, check with the host first to make sure a gratuity is appropriate.

Don't make other plans without letting your host know. An example: If your host lives in the same town as another friend whom you'd like to visit, you must tell your host before you arrive: "Madeline, I'm hoping to have time for a short visit with Sandra Dowd. Is that okay, or would it disrupt your plans?" If she says that's fine, ask her which day and time would be the best for seeing your friend.

Don't ask to bring your pet. This admonition

applies only for a host you don't know very well, whom you will put in a difficult position if she's unenthusiastic. With friends, go ahead and ask. If they say, "No problem," assure them that your pet's behavior will be exemplary—but only if it's true. If your pet is prone to chewing things or jumping onto furniture or into laps, arrange for it to be cared for while you're away.

Don't delay returning a borrowed item. Return it as soon as you no longer need it—and in as good shape, or even better than as when it was lent to you. Take care not to crease or stain the pages of a book, clean a clothes brush of lint, and switch any small appliances back to their original settings.

Don't accept an invitation before checking with your host. If you run into other friends in the area and they invite you (and perhaps your host as well) over for drinks or dinner, never accept the invitation before discussing the matter with those with whom you are staying.

Don't answer your host's telephone without asking. This rule applies even if you're right next to the phone. At the start of your stay, ask, "Jenny, do you want me to answer the phone when it rings, or should I let the answering machine pick up?"

You should also ask your host whether she wants to be told of any calls that come in while you're using the phone.

Don't use more than your share of hot water. In weekend houses with small hot water heaters—or in any house where you know a number of people will be bathing—keep your showers short. Other bathroom no-no's: Don't use any towels or washcloths other than those specified as your own, don't leave the bathmat in a wrinkled heap on the floor, and don't leave the toilet seat up.

Don't make the first move to go to bed. When to end the evening is the host's prerogative. You can hint that you're tired, but the custom is to wait for the host to give the signal. The exception is when your hosts are family or close friends who won't mind if you retire early or stay up late. Just conform to the host's habits as much as possible.

Don't leave without making sure you have all your belongings. The reading glasses hidden behind the lamp on the nightstand, the shoes left under the bed—wrapping up and mailing forgotten items is a chore for your host. Do a thorough check of your room or sleeping area, no matter how sure you are that you've packed everything.

GUIDELINES FOR GUESTS

Just as the good host should be clear when issuing an invitation, houseguests should be prompt with their replies and precise about their arrival times. Promptness is all the more important if the invitation is for a longer visit and you'll be one among several guests.

Replying to Invitations

Handwritten or e-mail replies should be sent right away, regardless of the nature of your visit (even your scatterbrained ex–college roommate probably books her appointments and social activities in advance). Include the time of your arrival and your means of transportation: "Dear Rhonda, what an exciting invitation! We plan to drive up by car and should arrive about 7 o'clock on Friday the 12th. Can't wait to see you and Bill. . . ."

If you receive a phoned invitation for a weekend party for several guests, don't say something like, "I'll have to find out about a job interview I've been waiting for. I'll let you know next week." If you can't give a definite answer within a day or two, it's better to refuse so that the host can fill your place with someone else.

Guests who are coming and going by plane or

train should always confirm their return reservations. No matter how successful the weekend party, it should end when the host expects it to (with the final day made clear in her invitation). Likewise, no guest should risk being put in the position of overstaying because he suddenly finds there are no seats left on the Sunday-night plane.

How to Leave the Bed

On the morning of the day you're going to leave, ask your hostess what she would like you to do with your bed linen, then follow her wishes. If you're uncertain what to do, standard practice is to remove the sheets, fold them, place them at the foot of the bed, and pull the blanket and spread up neatly so that the bed will look made. If you make it up with your sheets in place, it is all too easy for a busy hostess to forget, turning down the bedspread for the next guest only to find used sheets.

Should you make the bed with fresh sheets? That depends. If the two of you are only casual friends, your hostess may feel uncomfortable because she thinks such a task the duty of the host. But if you're close friends and you visit frequently, go ahead and ask for fresh sheets and save your host the trouble.

Saying "Thank You"

Overnight visits require handwritten thank-you notes—with the emphasis on "handwritten"—within a day or two of your return home. (The only exception is when your hosts are relatives or close friends who often visit you in return. Even then, a call the next day to say, "We're still talking about how fun the weekend was!" is appreciated.) E-mailing your thanks to anyone but your relatives and closest friends is inappropriate because it reduces the host's considerable effort on your behalf to the level of a casual lunch or a lift to work.

EXTENDED VISITS

Extended visits are almost entirely restricted to family members who come to stay for a week or more, often over a holiday. The following are a few guidelines for dealing with problems that may crop up over the course of a longish stay.

Tips for Hosts

> When, say, your mother is staying with you and you're invited somewhere, should you ask if you may bring her? In general, don't. For an invitation to dinner or any other occasion that requires the host to have an exact guest head-

count, you can say, "I'm afraid we can't come—Mother is staying with us." This leaves it up to the host whether to suggest that you bring your mother. When the invitation is to an open house, a cocktail party, or a church or club festivity, one more guest wouldn't cause any difficulty, so feel free to ask if you may bring someone else along.

➤ When an invitation to an event doesn't include your houseguest, it's up to you and your guest whether you should go, though in most cases it's better not to. If your guest is a close relative who's visiting for more than a few days, you might agree that it's fine for you to go alone. Just be sure he has something to do and to eat while you're away.

➤ Plan together how you and your guest will handle your routines (work, school, shopping, and so forth) and any special activities—together or separately?

➤ Arrange for use of a car if your guest needs one, or help with transportation plans.

➤ Offer your guest the use of your computer for e-mail and Internet access.

➢ Give your guests permission to use your washer and dryer whenever they like.

Tips for Guests

➢ Thoughtful guests make a point of immediately saying that no one needs to entertain them—then proving the point by finding things to do.

➢ It's disruptive when the guest follows the host from room to room or chats nonstop with a child who is trying to complete his homework.

➢ A thoughtful guest doesn't sit in on every conversation, but rather goes on a walk or to another room in the house so that the host family can have some private time together.

➢ A guest who has to stay longer than expected for business reasons, interviews, or other scheduled events should share his schedule with the host.

➢ Helping with routine activities (shopping, preparing a meal, or assisting the children with homework) helps keep the host's daily life from being unduly disrupted by the guest's extended stay.

Chapter Five

PARTIES GALORE

Parties can be as different as night and day. At one extreme is the informal gathering of shorts-wearing friends and neighbors at a backyard barbecue; at the other, the formal ball, with all its intricate planning and adherence to tradition. The requirements for a successful party of any kind, however, are precisely the same: Hosts do all they can to make their guests comfortable, and guests mind their manners by being both flexible and appreciative of their hosts' efforts.

Even the most carefree parties demand guests and hosts alike to meet certain expectations. The host must have planned sufficiently, and then look after the assembled partygoers to varying degrees. Guests should fit their behavior to the occasion, with the Party Animal calming down at a reserved affair, the Show-Off yielding the spotlight, and the Shrinking Violet making an effort to blossom.

Cocktail parties open this chapter, which then moves on to parties as varied as open houses, ultracasual parties, reunions, cooking parties, parties on the water, and formal balls. (See also Chapter 3, page 116: "The Dinner Party.")

A "CONGENIAL STEW" OF GUESTS

Today's best hosts and hostesses (for the sake of simplicity, hereafter referred to in this chapter as hosts) agree that the right mix of guests—a "congenial stew"—can make all the difference when holding a party. You might enjoy mixing and matching people who don't know one another but who you suspect will get on famously. Your primary goal is to invite guests who are likely to be interesting to one another and whom you can count on to be sensitive, thoughtful, and entertaining.

How to Invite

Party invitations range from a spontaneous, same-day phone call or e-mail ("My cousin Francesca is in town unexpectedly and we'd love it if you and Lawrence could join us for a barbecue tonight") to a formal engraved invitation to a charity ball sent well in advance.

When to Send?

Whether you're mailing printed invitations or

inviting guests by phone, timing is key. Send an invitation too late and the guest may already be booked; send it too early and it can be misplaced or forgotten.

The following guidelines aren't set in stone but will give you an idea of how to time invitations for different kinds of parties:

Anniversary party	3 to 6 weeks
Bar or bat mitzvah	1 month
Bon voyage party	Last minute to 3 weeks
Charity ball	6 weeks to 3 months
Christmas party	1 month
Cocktail party	1 to 4 weeks
Debutante ball	6 weeks to 3 months
Formal dinner	3 to 6 weeks
Graduation party	3 weeks
Housewarming party	Few days to 3 weeks
Informal dinner	Few days to 3 weeks
Lunch or tea	Few days to 2 weeks
Thanksgiving dinner	2 weeks to 2 months
Ultracasual party	Same day to 2 weeks

THE RETURN OF THE COCKTAIL PARTY

The new interest in cocktails (both classic and new) is only one reason cocktail parties have enjoyed a recent resurgence. Another is that they're the answer to a busy person's prayer, offering a simple solution to the rule that all invitations must be repaid. Cocktail parties also require less preparation than a dinner party, can be less expensive, have set time limits, and make it possible to entertain a lot of people in a small setting. On the minus side, guests don't have the "favored few" status they do at a dinner party, and the hosts' attention will be spread thin.

Please Come For . . .

Cocktail parties can be large or small and as simple or elaborate as you wish. For a small or last-minute party, it's fine to invite by phone. For a larger party, invitations on fill-in cards are the better choice.

A cocktail party invitation typically specifies a set time: "Cocktails from 5:00 to 7:00." If you're planning a cocktail buffet—a cross between a cocktail party and a buffet dinner—your invitation need only state the arrival time: "Cocktail buffet at 6:30."

"Cocktail buffet" in the invitation tells guests that more than snacks will be provided. Although you needn't set out a soup-to-nuts buffet, guests should have enough food so that they won't need to make dinner plans for later.

Some hosts choose to leave RSVP off the invitation, especially if the party is a big one. For one thing, they could be inundated with phone calls (the usual way to respond to parties of this kind); for another, cocktail buffets don't need the exact guest count normally required for dinner parties. Whether to add an RSVP notation is your decision.

Advice for the Host

When hosting a cocktail party, stock your liquor cabinet with the basics: Scotch, bourbon, a blended whiskey, gin, vodka, rum, white and red wine, and beer. If you know several guests are partial to martinis or Bloody Marys, stock up accordingly.

Also make sure nondrinkers have a range of juices, soft drinks, and bottled waters to choose from. A smart host will have enough supplies (especially ice) on hand, mix drinks correctly but moderately, and set out plenty of coasters and napkins.

Hors d'oeuvres are the only food served unless you're hosting a cocktail buffet (see Chapter 3, page 126: "Cocktail buffet"). Virtually any finger food will do as long as it tastes good, looks tempting, and can be eaten with little fuss. The hors d'oeuvres are usually served on a buffet table (and sometimes passed on trays), but it's also a good idea to have bowls of snacks placed around the room—nuts, chips, pretzels, olives, and the like.

If you and your spouse or partner are acting not only as hosts but as bartenders and servers as well, follow your greeting to a guest with an offer to get him a drink. If the choice of beverages is limited, save embarrassment all around by asking, "Will you have a martini, wine, beer, or juice?"—not "What would you like?"

You can also invite your guests to refill their own glasses if they want another drink. Just be sure to have the beverages, a jigger, and a bucket of ice in clear view. A self-serve bar will help free up your time to visit and perform other duties.

At a large cocktail party, guests expect to stand for long periods, but you still should provide enough chairs for those who need to rest. When the guest list is small (say, six to ten), people are more likely to gravitate to chairs and couches, so make sure there are enough seats for everyone present.

SIX WAYS TO BE A GOOD HOST

No matter the kind of party you're throwing, there are some things a host should remember, even before the party starts.

Invite clearly. Include necessary information for your guests in the invitation. Is the party a casual get-together or more formal? What about the attire? Maybe a guest would benefit by knowing ahead of time who else will be there, which you might mention when they RSVP.

Plan well. Preparing your guest list carefully is key to a successful party. Then do as much as you can ahead of time. (Lower the stress level by serving food and refreshments you know will work.) Get everything ready well before your guests arrive, so you'll feel relaxed from the very beginning.

Remain calm. Giving a party can be enjoyable, especially if you approach it with simplicity. Get help if necessary, and don't let your guests think you're huffing and puffing. They'll feel far more comfortable if they don't have to wonder whether they're causing you any trouble.

Keep guests feeling welcome. Make sure guests are warmly greeted, then made to feel welcome throughout the party. Look after each guest as much as you can. If you notice that a guest has an empty glass or if there's one person standing alone, remedy the situation as quickly and cheerfully as possible.

> ***Be flexible and gracious.*** Your soufflé falls. Or
> one friend arrives with an unexpected guest. The
> ruined dessert? Have a fallback. The uninvited
> guest? As discourteous as it is for someone to
> spring a surprise on you, be gracious. No polite
> host would ever send an uninvited guest packing.
>
> ***Be appreciative.*** Thank people for coming as you
> bid them good-bye. And don't forget to thank any-
> one who brought you a gift.

Need Hired Help?

When you're planning a cocktail party for more
than twenty people, it's wise to hire a bartender for
the evening, if possible. If the guest list is in the
forty-to-fifty range, two bartenders would be needed, with their tables set up in two different places
to prevent a crush at the bar.

Be sure that you instruct the bartender how you
want the drinks mixed and tell her to rely on a
jigger or other measure. If you let her pour by eye,
you may find your liquor supply running out long
before you'd planned. (You might also have some
unexpectedly boisterous guests on your hands!) Ask
your bartender to wrap a napkin around each glass,
whether a fresh drink or a refill. Napkins prevent

drips and make holding a wet, icy glass more comfortable.

The Art of Mingling

If as a guest you find yourself on the sidelines, don't be embarrassed to introduce yourself to someone. When the person is alone, the introduction is easy. More difficult is joining a group conversation. To smooth the way, walk past to see what is being discussed. (Not that you want to eavesdrop, but this is a party, where mixing is desirable.) If the subject is sports, computers, a current news story, or any other impersonal topic, you've found a conversation open to all. Smile and make eye contact with one or two people, and wait for someone to acknowledge your presence. Then listen patiently and wait for a lull before joining in. If, on the other hand, the subject is personal or about people you don't know, move on.

Juggling Acts

How on earth do you juggle your drink and your plate and shake hands at the same time? Only with great difficulty, so try to find a place to set one of the items down.

Standing close to a table could solve the problem. Just make sure the table isn't set or decorated in such a way that even the temporary addition of a wineglass spoils the effect or your dish could be confused with whatever is being served. Another option: Some people are poised enough to joke about their dilemma, asking someone to hold their glass while they extend their hand. The important thing is to make the effort to greet another person in a pleasant way.

What to do with toothpicks after you've eaten an hors d'oeuvre? There's usually a small receptacle on or near the food platter for used ones. If not, hold any items (including drink stirrers) in your napkin until you find a wastebasket. Don't place used items on the buffet table unless a waste receptacle is available.

The Tipsy Guest

The guest who drinks too much at a party used to be laughed off later as "the guy who put a lampshade on his head" or "swung from the chandeliers"—but when anyone who's inebriated plans to drive home, overindulgence no longer raises even a smile.

When it becomes obvious that one of the guests has had too much, the host or the person tending bar should not serve him more liquor. The guest may be insulted and become abusive, but that is preferable to having him become more intoxicated.

As the host, you are responsible for seeing that a

drunken guest is taken safely home. You may ask a good friend to take him; you can go yourself if the inebriated person's home is close by; or you can arrange for a cab. The person's car keys should be taken away if he is not willing to go with someone else. If he has reached the stage of almost passing out, two or three of the other guests should help him to a bed to sleep it off overnight. If the offender has a spouse or a date present, the host and hostess should offer this person accommodations or see that he or she gets safely home.

"Would You Please Leave Your Shoes at the Door?"

While removing your shoes when entering someone else's home isn't typically a part of U.S. culture, as it is in Japan and elsewhere, politely asking family, friends, and party guests to do so is fine — especially in locales with long seasons of inclement weather. Just make sure you have a stash of comfortable slippers, flip-flops, or nonskid slippers or socks for visitors to wear. That way, guests won't feel so uncomfortable about exposing their bare or stocking feet. Be careful, though. If you're throwing a more formal party or you don't know your guests all that well, asking them to remove their shoes could be awkward.

THE ULTRACASUAL PARTY

Some gatherings are so casual they hardly qualify as parties: the after-work get-together at a coworker's apartment, the impromptu invitation for a few neighbors to "drop by this evening," the occasional gatherings with a group of close friends. Many of these parties are potlucks, with each guest bringing a dish or a sweet.

While most of the rules for a "real" party can be suspended—the only written invitation would be one delivered via e-mail, and "anything goes" attire is fine as long as it's not sloppy or too revealing—there are still a few hosting duties to perform. First, make sure the party area, kitchen, and bathroom are clean, and close off any messy rooms. Unless the party is both a potluck and BYOB, estimate how much food and alcohol to buy, and stock the fridge with soft drinks and sparkling water to accommodate nondrinkers. Vary the choice of food (whether hors d'oeuvres or a buffet) so that all the guests will find something to their taste.

Paper napkins are the sensible choice for very casual parties, with large colored ones more festive than plain white. If no buffet is being served, a stack of smaller cocktail or luncheon-sized napkins will be sufficient.

Sturdy paper or plastic plates, plastic utensils, and disposable cups are not only in keeping with the spirit of the affair but also make cleanup easier. If you're using your own dinnerware and utensils, there's no need to match styles and patterns.

Party Time

When guests arrive, it's fine to have someone else open the door for them if you're occupied, but do make a point to greet them as soon as possible. If it's coat season and you don't have a coat closet, either direct guests to a bed where coats, jackets, and handbags are being piled or take the items to the bedroom yourself. Make sure clothing doesn't end up in a crumpled heap and won't be covered with pet hair.

As guests arrive, ask what they'd like to drink. As you hand them their drinks, tell them that they're welcome to help themselves from the countertop, refrigerator, or ice chest—or, if the party is large, perhaps from the ice-filled "cooler" that is your bathtub—for the rest of the party.

Have plenty of large garbage bags handy so you can periodically collect empty cans or used paper plates and stash them out of sight. Wash glasses and other dishes as needed, or let guests take on the task if they volunteer.

When guests leave, show them to the door and tell them how much you enjoyed their company—one nicety that should never be ignored.

OPEN-HOUSE PARTIES

Most open houses—parties where guests can arrive anytime between the hours specified in the invitation—are usually held after the host has moved into a new home or to celebrate a holiday. Depending on the degree of informality (open houses can be quite casual), you may send written invitations or commercial cards or invite people by phone. Some hosts include an RSVP or "Regrets only," while others are willing to guess about the final number of guests.

Refreshments range from the simple—dips, sandwiches, bowls of nuts or olives, and punch—to elaborate buffets of country hams, hot biscuits, cheese puffs, and bowls of shrimp. Guests generally stay no longer than an hour or hour and a half so that the crowd won't balloon to unmanageable proportions.

HOUSEWARMINGS

If you've recently moved to a new house, you might choose to host a housewarming, typically a cocktail party or buffet. Depending on the casualness of the party, you can send written invitations, phone your friends, or e-mail them.

Expect to give tours unless you're comfortable letting guests wander through the house on their own. Just make sure someone is always there to open the front door and welcome guests as you play tour guide.

Gifts are often brought to a housewarming party. If the group is small enough and every guest has brought a gift, opening the presents can be a part of the festivities. If the party is more of an open house, with guests coming and going, either open each gift and thank the guest as it's given or wait until after the party—in which case a thank-you note is a must. Even if someone has been directly thanked for a gift at the party, a thank-you note is a good idea—and always appreciated.

Typical gifts are guest towels, place mats, houseplants, drinking glasses, nice dishcloths or napkins, and (for the host who gardens) spring bulbs and seeds. Other ideas include a guest book intended as a keepsake of the party; a picture frame (take a photo in front of their new home to add later); and tickets or discount coupons to local movie theaters, restaurants, or shops.

SIX WAYS TO BE A GOOD GUEST

Even at the most casual parties, there are some things a polite guest should do:

Tell your host whether you're attending. And do it immediately. If you delay your reply, you could hinder the host's planning and also make it seem as if you're waiting for something better to come along. Even if no RSVP has been requested, it's thoughtful to let your host know if you won't be able to be there.

Be on time. Punctuality means different things to people in different locales, but in general guests should arrive at or shortly after (usually only fifteen minutes) the time stated on the invitation. Do *not*, however, arrive early.

Be a willing participant. When your host says that it's time for dinner, go straight to the table. If you happen to be asked to participate in a party game or view Susie's graduation pictures, accept graciously and enthusiastically no matter how you really feel.

Offer to help when you can. If you're visiting with the host in the kitchen as he prepares the food, be specific when you offer to help: "I'd be happy to work on the salad or fill the water glasses." Even if your offer is refused, your gesture will be appreciated. When the party's end draws nigh, you could also offer to help with the cleanup.

Don't overindulge. Attacking finger foods as if you haven't eaten in a week will not only attract the wrong kind of attention, it will also leave less food for other guests. Also be sure to keep any consumption of alcoholic beverages on the moderate to low side.

Thank the host twice. In some parts of the United States, a second thank-you by phone is customary the day after the party (the first having been delivered on leaving the party)—a gesture that's gracious anywhere. If the party was formal, written thanks are in order. In fact, a written note is always appreciated—even after very casual parties.

COMMON INTEREST PARTIES

Friends who share a common interest often set up regular gatherings to discuss books, cook, quilt or knit, or even watch a favorite show or sports event on TV. Hosting is usually rotated among the members, and refreshments are served—either during the activity or afterward, as common sense demands.

If such gatherings have any etiquette guidelines in common, they are to pay attention to the subject at hand, avoid getting into arguments, and respect the opinions of others.

Book Groups

Friends and acquaintances who form a book club draw up a reading list and discuss a book after everyone has read it, usually meeting once a month. The behavior guidelines are straightforward: Listen when others are talking and take care not to interrupt. Respect the viewpoints of others, and don't leave the impression that your interpretation of the author's work is the correct one and somebody else's is wrong.

Cooking Groups

Serious cooks who meet regularly get the chance to try out new gourmet dishes, taste a variety of wines, and have a great time in the bargain. A certain cuisine—say, Italian, Mexican, or Thai—is often chosen, and club members, who usually number six to twelve, are assigned certain dishes to prepare. The party is held at a different member's home each time the group meets, and the host is usually responsible for sodas, coffee, tea, mixers, condiments, and the table setting. Depending on the space in the host's kitchen, dishes can either be made ahead or prepared on site, with various members offering to pitch in as others look on while relaxing and sipping wine.

Constructive criticism of the dishes is part of the point of such parties, but criticizing a cook's skills is out of bounds. Be sure to help with the cleanup, and thank the host just as you would after any party.

Craft Groups

Friends who enjoy quilting, needlework, leather-work, or any other craft have fun working on their individual projects together, but their parties could also have a purpose—making items for a hospital, nursery, or other organization. Members of the group take turns hosting and should have some extra project supplies on hand in case they're need-ed. During the session, criticism of another person's work should be constructive, of course, and everyone should pitch in to clean up at the party's end.

A QUESTION FOR PEGGY

My wife and I threw a party last weekend, and to our surprise one couple stayed after everyone else had left. I tried dropping a hint by saying we had to get our six-year-old to a bus for a field trip at the crack of dawn, but it went right over their heads. How should I have handled the situation?

Be glad that your party was such fun that guests wanted to linger. Still, it's okay to let guests know it's time to go. Just be honest, saying how much you've enjoyed their visit but that you have to get up early for work (or whatever the case may be).

To prevent the problem, send a signal as the party draws to a close. One way is to ask, "Would anyone like a nightcap? Some coffee?" Once the drinks and last refreshments have been served, start tidying up a little. If most people soon begin to leave, you could ask someone who stays firmly planted in his chair, "Dan, shall I bring your coat?" Or you could be pleasantly blunt: "Dan, I'm going to have to kick you out in fifteen minutes, since I have a six o'clock flight tomorrow morning"—an explanation that asks for Dan's understanding, gives him a chance to finish a drink or a conversation, and depart as though it were his idea in the first place.

FORMAL PARTIES

Those opulent balls familiar to us from the movies—men in tails swirling elegantly gowned women around the floor to the strains of a Strauss waltz—may have gone the way of the dance card, but they are echoed in today's formal dances, be they club dances, school formals, corporate events of one kind or another, or charity or debutante balls.

Unlike the grand parties of old, large formal parties are usually hosted by a committee. Special duties are allotted to each member of the committee, with one taking charge of invitations, one of decorations, another of the food, and so forth.

The Party Begins

Once you've arrived, you'll most likely begin the evening with pre-dinner drinks and hors d'oeuvres served from a bar, buffet tables, trays carried by waiters who circulate through the room, or a combination thereof. A guest's concerns at this phase:

THE BAR. If there is no true bar on the premises, bartenders will serve from a table, mixing drinks or pouring wine or beer. Before ordering, be certain it's your turn; if in doubt, a gracious "You go first" will be well received.

Waiters may be serving wine, passing through the room with trays. Don't make a beeline to a waiter; either wait patiently until the waiter comes your way or go stand in line at the drinks table or bar. Take a napkin and keep it wrapped around the base of your glass. Remember to keep the drink in your left hand so that your right one is ready for handshakes. When your glass is empty, look for a sideboard or table where used glasses and plates are deposited; if you can't find one, ask a waiter or the bartender what to do with your glass.

Don't tip the bartender unless there's a cash bar, in which case you will pay for your drinks—an arrangement unlikely at most formal affairs, but a possibility. Gratuities are built into the waitstaff's fees, so leaving money on the table or tray puts bartenders and waiters in an awkward position.

PASSED-TRAY SERVICE. When taking food from a passed tray, try not to bring the food directly to your mouth; instead, put it on your plate or napkin before picking it up to eat. Also remember not to eat, talk, and drink at the same time.

A BUFFET TABLE. When hors d'oeuvres are set on a buffet table, guests pick up plates and help themselves to both finger foods and dishes that require a fork. Take small portions, and don't return for plateful after plateful; the food at this stage of the party should take a backseat to the people around you.

FOOD STATIONS. Food stations are smaller tables set in strategic locations around the room, each holding a different kind of food—ethnic specialties, perhaps, or all vegetarian dishes. Try not to frequent only one; other guests may be just as fond of Mexican food as you are, and you don't want to be responsible for the sudden dearth of empanadas.

Dress for a Ball

"Black tie" (tuxedo) is accepted at most balls, even if the invitation says "formal"; only if the invitation specifies "white tie" must a man wear white tie and tails.

For women, dresses are usually long. A ball is also the time to wear your finest jewelry. Pants on women are acceptable only if they are very full and styled to look like a ball gown. With sleeveless or strapless gowns, women may wear long gloves, which they leave on through the beginning of the ball but remove when they begin dancing or eating.

"SHALL WE DANCE?"

These days, women don't have to be asked to dance but instead can take the initiative and ask men. If in doubt about the appropriateness, just remember that the more formal the party, the more you should stick to tradition. Speaking of formal, tradition says that every man at a private ball should dance with the hostess and the women he sits between at dinner, but he dances the first dance of the evening with his wife or date.

Today's dancing etiquette is otherwise based on common sense:

➢ Don't come to the party wearing too much perfume or cologne.

➢ If the dance floor is crowded, dance in compact steps and keep your arms in.

➢ If you bump someone, say, "So sorry!"

➢ Don't correct or criticize your partner on the dance floor.

➢ Execute any drops, flips, lifts, or turns only when you have plenty of space (yes, swing is back).

Time was when a man could cut in on a couple by tapping the man's shoulder and then taking over as the woman's dance partner. Today, this custom is largely confined to avid dancers of a certain age and to young teens thrilling to their first dance parties.

Receiving Lines

The members of a receiving line include the host and hostess at a private ball, the committee heads at a public ball, and honored guests (a debutante, for example) and their escorts. At a large function, this may be the only time a guest is able to say hello to the hosts and thank them for the party.

It's fine for a guest to hold a drink while waiting to be received, but the glass and any food should be disposed of before he or she goes through the line. When the moment arrives, the guest shakes hands and briefly exchanges a few pleasant words with each member of the line.

Midnight Supper or Breakfast

Since most balls begin well after the dinner hour, a late buffet supper (or "breakfast") is often served; it begins after midnight and continues for an hour or more. Food might consist of a variety of sandwiches, platters of cold meats and assorted vegetables, or eggs with bacon or ham. There may be hot drinks, bowls of iced fruit punch, or champagne.

People may serve themselves whenever they feel like it, and small tables are usually provided. Guests can sit where they please—in any vacant chairs or with a group making up a table.

When you're ready to leave a formal ball (usually after the supper, though older people often leave before midnight), find the host and hostess and thank them, just as you would at a smaller party. If there's a guest of honor, you should say good-bye to him or her as well.

PARTY AHOY!

A harbor, lake, river, or coastline provides the opportunity for another party locale: a boat. A boat owner might enjoy entertaining friends on a day cruise or an evening sunset sail. Other hosts might want to book a party boat that plies local waters. Still others may prefer a historic vessel moored at a jetty—the kind that a number of river towns and harborside cities have turned into party boats outfitted with dining rooms and reception rooms. (Old paddle steamers are popular in the South.)

An invitation to an on-the-water party should

make clear whether it is on a moored boat or one that will cruise. Dinner cruises are popular, especially in cities where the skyline forms a glittering backdrop. But a party boat that sets sail brings a new set of concerns. Because people are unable to leave when they choose, the cruise should be kept to two hours or less; this way, the partygoers won't start feeling trapped or end up drinking more than they should. In any case, it's wise to stock up on nonalcoholic drinks. Seasickness medicine should also be available on board should the waters turn choppy.

If you're hosting a party on your own boat, be sure to follow boating safety rules (including having the correct number of life vests on board), and don't forget to orient your guests to the layout of the boat, pointing out the location of the galley and the head.

At Debutante Balls

The phrase "presenting a debutante to society" has seen its day. Today a debutante ball is a celebration of a young woman's "coming of age" (somewhere between her eighteenth and twenty-third birthday) at a formal ball or party. Celebratory customs vary

around the country, with the age of the debutante
and the rituals of the ball or party differing from
place to place.

The most elaborate party is a private ball.
Somewhat less elaborate is a small dance; less
elaborate still is a tea dance. Often, a dance is given
for, or by, the families of several debutantes. Or the
dance could be given by an organization that
invites a group of girls to participate. Many balls or
cotillions of this kind are benefits, handled by a
committee representing the sponsoring charity.
Thus these balls serve a double purpose, since the
parents of the girls invited to participate are
sometimes expected to give a substantial donation
to the charity in return for the privilege of having
their daughters presented.

Whether the party is a ball or dance, the
debutante's mother—or grandmother or whoever is
giving the party and "presenting" the debutante—
stands near the entrance. The debutantes stand
next to them, each debutante paired with her
mother or other presenter. The debutantes and
their mothers (or other presenters) are the only
people who formally "receive." On entering, the
guests approach the hostesses, who introduce the
debutantes to those who don't know the young
women being presented.

Each debutante receives guests for about an hour, after which she's free to enjoy the dancing. She usually dances the first dance with her father and the next with the man (or men) she's asked to be her escort(s) for the evening. The debutante then goes to supper with her escort(s). She will have decided in advance who will join her at the table reserved for her group.

THE DEBUTANTE'S DRESS. The debutante traditionally wears a white gown. While a pastel color or a color in the trim of the gown is acceptable, scarlet, bright blue, and black are inappropriate. When the ball is an assembly or cotillion, the committee determines the color of the debutantes' gowns, a decision that must be followed. Although they must wear the same color, the young women may choose their own styles. Long white gloves are worn during the presentation.

PARENTS' AND GUESTS' ATTIRE. The mothers of the debutantes wear evening dresses in any color except white or black, while female guests wear evening dresses in any color other than white. Traditionally, long gloves are worn, unless a woman's dress is long-sleeved. Male guests' attire is black tie, but the escorts and the fathers of the debutantes usually wear white tie.

FLOWERS AND GIFTS. It's customary for family members and very close friends to send flowers (whether bouquets or baskets) to the home of the debutante at the time of her coming-out party. The debutante's escort(s) may also send flowers and give her a corsage if one will be worn—but they should ask before doing so. Young women often don't wear flowers on their gowns but instead pin them to a purse or wear them on the wrist.

Relatives and very close friends of the debutante or her family can also send gifts, though this isn't required. Members of the organizing committee and guests of the family can also send gifts if they wish.

"PLEASE JOIN US FOR A REUNION . . ."

Reunions are parties with a built-in plus—the opportunity to catch up with old friends or to reunite with family members who live far away. Reunions can be held by anyone, from former workmates to military buddies, and class reunions are a long-standing custom. Each has its own unofficial code of conduct.

CLASS REUNIONS. High school and college reunions hold a special place in the American psyche. To many people, they're the time to proudly show who they've become (the unpopular boy who became a business tycoon, the gangly girl who's now a model). To others, they're a chance to revisit old times and revive friendships. In any event, keep the following advice in mind:

➤ *Invite everyone.* Unless close friends who keep in touch want to plan their own mini-reunion, the planners of a class reunion should invite every member of the class. If someone can't be tracked down through mailings, phone calls, and Internet searches, that's that. But no planner should fail to invite someone because "she wouldn't want to come anyway"—or for any other reason.

➤ *Don't just stick with your old crowd.* Make a point to greet and chat with as many classmates as possible. After all, that's the point of the party!

➤ *Forgo the bragging.* The need to impress can backfire. If you go on and on about your accomplishments, your great job, or your brilliant and beautiful children, your boasting will overshadow your successes. Counter the urge to brag by expressing interest in others.

➤ *Make others feel included.* If a classmate seems to be hanging back or spends too much time alone, walk over and strike up a conversation. If you feel someone has been left out of the conviviality, ask him or her to dance when the opportunity arises.

➢ *Don't be scornful.* Don't scorn the city or town where someone lives or what they do for a living. People want different things out of life, and your attitude should be one of approval of the road they've taken.

➢ *Don't embarrass classmates.* Don't bring up incidents they would probably rather forget, no matter how funny they may be. What's a fond memory for some may be anything but for others.

➢ *Thank the planners of the event.* They volunteered their valuable time, and their reward is their classmates' appreciation and the satisfaction that a good time was had by all.

FAMILY REUNIONS. In some U.S. families, what was often a one-day picnic to bring together relatives from far and wide often ballons into a weekend gathering with scheduled events and entertainment. The etiquette guidelines for family reunions apply no matter how long or elaborate the gathering.

➢ *Provide a range of activities.* Just because

people are related doesn't mean they share the same interests. Everybody might enjoy a sack race or a game of tug-of-war, but others will appreciate having a golf, bowling, or softball game scheduled as well. Sightseeing trips and shopping excursions can be scheduled as alternatives.

➤ *Watch your manners.* You should never suspend the social graces just because you're with family. Use the same good manners you would with a group of friends or total strangers, whether dining, socializing, or competing in a congenial game.

➤ *Respect the organizer.* Don't complain about the way the reunion was organized, which does nothing more than make you look petty. Perhaps you would have done things differently, but accept the party for what it is and thank the organizers for their hard work.

➤ *Don't get into one-upmanship.* Competing with relatives over whose children are the more outstanding or whose job outshines whose introduces a sour note to the festivities. You can mention your child's or your own latest accomplishments, but take care not to brag. Always ask about the other person's children or work, show interest, and give praise where praise is due.

➢ *Zip your lip.* Don't spread gossip about any family member(s), and keep any personal or family secrets to yourself. A confessional to a relative can either wait until another time or be suspended altogether.

➢ *Don't be disapproving of other people's children.* Criticizing the behavior of a relative's child is as bad an idea at a reunion as commenting on the behavior of a stranger's child in a supermarket. Mothers and fathers won't be any less sensitive about criticism of their parenting abilities just because it comes from a relative.

➢ *Spread a little sunshine.* Let your relatives know when you particularly like something about them. Don't fawn over anyone, but give compliments where compliments are due and tell people how much it means to you to get to know them better.

Chapter Six

TOASTS AND TOASTING

Toasts range from the most routine ("To us!" spoken while clinking glasses) to the most touching—a five-minute homage from the father of the bride that could make grown men cry. In one form or another, toasting to love, friendship, health, wealth, and happiness has been practiced by almost every culture from the beginning of recorded history. The Greeks and the Romans, the potentates of Africa and Asia, and the indigenous peoples of South America and the Pacific Islands all drank to their gods, as did the Europeans— notably, the Vikings, who used the skulls (*skalle*) of their vanquished foes as goblets. That singular custom gave rise to the standard Scandinavian toast: *Skål*.

WHO TOASTS—AND WHEN

In years past, it was the prerogative of the host or hostess to offer the first toast, whether at a small dinner party or a soirée. Nowadays, the more informal the occasion, the less this "rule" applies: Around a dinner table with friends, a guest can propose the first toast (and often does), usually as a way of thanking the host for bringing everyone together. The only real guideline is to make sure that all the glasses are filled before toasting. The glasses don't have to hold champagne or wine or any other alcoholic beverage; it's perfectly fine for nondrinkers to toast with water, juice, or a soft drink. Even an empty glass is better than nothing. It's the gesture and warm wishes, not the alcohol, that really matter.

The "host toasts first" mandate *does* still apply at receptions and other large functions (though the best man usually leads the toasting at a wedding reception). It is also the responsibility of the host to attract the crowd's attention when the time comes, which he does by standing and raising his glass—not by banging on a glass with a utensil. No matter how large and noisy the crowd, repeating "May I have your attention" as often as necessary is the more courteous option.

When it comes to sitting or standing, do what comes naturally. If toasts are made over pre-dinner drinks in the living room, the toaster may want to stand. At the dinner table, the toaster may remain seated if the group is fairly small. A table of a dozen or more usually requires the toaster to stand so that people will be able to hear.

Although the host often stands as he delivers his toast, everyone else—including the person or persons being toasted—remains seated. The exception is when the toaster asks everyone assembled to "rise and drink to the happy couple" or "stand and raise your glasses to our esteemed leader." The guests respond by taking a sip of their drinks, not by draining the glass; the idea is to save enough of the beverage for any toasts that follow. On ceremonial occasions, a toastmaster or the chairman of the committee often takes charge, sandwiching the necessary toasts between the end of the meal and before any speeches. Toasters are usually expected to stand on such formal occasions.

When to Toast

If a toast is to be offered at a meal, the first usually comes at the very beginning. Traditionally, the first toast is offered by the host as a welcome to guests. Toasts offered by others start during the dessert course.

Toasting isn't confined to a meal or special event. Spontaneous toasts are in order whenever they seem appropriate, as when someone raises his glass and offers good wishes or congratulations to his companions.

THE ORIGINS OF "TOAST"

Ironically, the cheerful clinking of a friend's glass before drinking evolved from one of the darker practices of the distant past. The custom dates back to the Middle Ages, when people were so distrustful of one another that they weren't above poisoning anyone they perceived as an enemy. As a safeguard, drinkers first poured a bit of wine into each other's glass, acting as mutual "tasters." Trustworthy friends, however, soon dispensed with the tastings and merely clinked their glasses instead. This custom is said by some to explain why "to your health" is the most common toast worldwide. Some other historians hold that clinking glasses provided the noise that would keep evil spirits at bay.

And the word "toast"? In the ale houses of Elizabethan England, a bit of spiced toast was usually put in the bottom of a cup of ale or wine to flavor it, and possibly to soak up the dregs. In time, any male or female whose qualities or accomplishments were frequently honored with a group drink came to be called "toasts" (hence the phrase "toast of the town"). One story—attributed, in a 1706 edition of *The Tatler*, to "many Wits of the last Age"—claimed that "toast" was first used in this manner during the reign of Charles II (1660–1684). That label, it was said, was bestowed on a well-known belle from the town of Bath. As the beauty luxuriated in the healthful waters of the public baths, an admiring gentleman scooped a little bath water into a cup, added the customary piece of toast, and raised the cupful of water to her before drinking it.

The word "toast" as used today—"a sentiment expressed just before drinking to someone"—did not begin to gain currency until the early 1700s.

Replying to a Toast

When toasted, the "toastee" does not stand, nor does she drink to herself. All the recipient need do is sit and smile appreciatively. Once the toast is finished, she simply acknowledges the toast with a "thank you." She may then stand and raise her own glass to propose a toast to the host or anyone else she wants to honor. The same procedure is followed by a group of people who have just been toasted.

Prepared Toasts

Anyone who wants to deliver more than the simplest toast should prepare beforehand, if only to rehearse mentally so as not to fumble the words. Keep whatever you say short and to the point—you want the spotlight to be on the toastee, not you. If, however, your toast has been designated as the principal one of the event, think of it as a small speech that should be prepared and rehearsed. When you deliver the toast, a glance at your notes is acceptable, but you still want to seem fairly spontaneous.

Including a few personal remarks—a reminiscence, praise, or a relevant story or joke—is all to the good, but they should be in keeping with the occasion. Toasts at a wedding should tend toward the sentimental, those in honor of a retiring employee toward nostalgia, and so forth. And a touch of humor is rarely out of place.

Spur-of-the-moment Toasts

Joining in a group toast is blessedly easy, with glasses raised and shouts of "Cheers!" "To your health!" or "To Stan!" ringing out. Similarly, a spontaneous toast is relatively effortless. It can be both brief and generic: "To Stan—God bless him!"

Should you draw a blank when you're suddenly asked to offer a toast, just remind yourself that a few sincere and complimentary words are all you need: "To Stan, a terrific guy and a friend to us all!" It's easier still when you can tie the toast to the occasion (what a good toaster should do in any event), whether you're at a dinner party or barbecue, an office party or a gathering of your high school classmates. In a pinch, try toasts along the lines of these:

"To Suzanne—a great hostess and a fabulous cook."

"To Dan—Cincinnati's best . . . and soon to be most famous? . . . barbecuer."

"To Paul—the host with the most!"

"To Gretchen—a great boss and a wonderful friend."

"To the class of '72—the smartest and best-looking by far!"

A TOAST SAMPLER

The following toasts are intended to give you a few ideas for various occasions, from weddings to holidays to housewarmings. Use the samples as a framework on which you build toasts that fit the toastee(s) and express your own feelings. Be sincere. You don't need to make it long; some of the most memorable toasts are brief. In some cases, you might choose to insert an appropriate proverb or saying, so a few of these are provided here as well.

Wedding Toasts

Weddings and the events surrounding them elicit so many toasts from well-wishers that whole books are devoted to the subject. But there's no reason to feel intimidated. As with all toasts, it's more important for the sentiments to be heartfelt than eloquent.

ENGAGEMENT PARTY TOASTS. In days past, a party was often held to announce an engagement. Today, engagement parties are usually a way for friends of the bride and groom to meet the couple's respective families a few months before the big event.

Parent(s) to couple

➢ "I [or we] propose that we all drink to the health and happiness of Keiran and the woman that he, to our great joy, is adding permanently to our family: Candace Roe."

➢ "Candace's mother and I have always looked forward to meeting the man she would choose to marry. I have to say we couldn't be happier with her choice—wonderful Keiran Matthews. Please join me in wishing them a long and happy marriage."

Bride and groom to future in-laws

➢ "Bill and Daphne [or Mr. and Mrs. Matthews], I'm so happy you're finally able to lay eyes on the friends I've been telling you about. It also gives *them* the chance to get to know *you*—a couple for whom I have the greatest respect and whose family I will be proud to join. Everyone, please join me in toasting Bill and Daphne Matthews!"

➢ "I remember the first time Candace took me to meet her parents. They quickly bowled me over with their hospitality, good cheer, and great sense of humor. Please join me in toasting two people whom I not only look forward to having as in-laws but as lifelong friends. To Ken and Fiona [or Mr. and Mrs. Roe]!"

REHEARSAL DINNER TOASTS. The rehearsal dinner—usually held after the wedding-eve rehearsal for the bride and groom, their families, attendants, and selected friends—allows any guest present the opportunity to toast the happy couple and others.

Parents to parents

➢ "I'd like to ask you to join me in toasting two wonderful people without whom this wedding could never have been possible: the mother and father of our soon-to-be daughter-in-law, Lynne—Mr. and Mrs. Brown."

Parents to couple

➢ "I don't need to tell you what a terrific person Lynne is, but I do want to tell you how happy Brett's mother and I are to welcome her as our new daughter-in-law. Here's to Lynne and Brett!"

Best man to groom

➢ "Brett and I have been friends for what seems like a lifetime now, and I've always noticed what a lucky guy he is. Tonight, all of you can see just what I mean as you look at Lynne. Please join me in a toast to both of them. May their lucky numbers keep coming up for the rest of their lives."

WEDDING RECEPTION TOASTS. Traditionally, the best man offers the first toast. Friends should keep their toasts to three or four minutes at the most, which will give family members and other attendants more time to propose their own.

Best man or maid of honor to couple

➢ After a brief speech, the head attendant could propose the toast by saying, "To Rosemary and John—extraordinary individuals in their own right. May they enjoy happiness and prosperity their whole lives long," or "To Rosemary and John— may they always be as happy as they are today."

Groom to bride; bride to groom

➢ "All my life I've wondered what the woman I'd marry would be like. In my wildest dreams, I never could've imagined she would be as fantastic as Keisha. Please join me in drinking this first toast to my beautiful bride."

➢ "I'd like you all to join me in a toast to the man who's just made me the happiest woman in the world. To Michael!"

Parents to couple

➢ "We're thrilled you're now a part of our family, and we know that Matt's [or Sherry's] life will be blessed and enriched by having you as his [her] wife [husband]. Matt and Sherry, we wish you health, wealth, and lifelong happiness as you set off on your greatest adventure."

➤ "As long as I've known Sherry, she's kept the perfect man in her mind's eye. And the first time I met Matt, I knew immediately that she had found him. Kids, you were no doubt meant for each other, and I want to wish you a long and happy life together."

➤ "Love does not consist in gazing at each other, but in looking outward in the same direction." (Antoine de Saint-Exupéry)

Anniversary Toasts

Whether part of a large anniversary party or made over an informal family dinner, toasts add to the gaiety of the occasion.

Friends to couple

➤ "Many of us can well remember that day twenty-five years ago when we drank a toast to Ann and Roger. It's obvious that our good wishes have served them well, so I'd like to ask everyone—old friends and new—to stand and raise your glasses to another twenty-five years of the same."

Children to couple

➤ "Mom and Dad, how can we ever thank you? You not only built a home full of life and love but you also equipped Edith and me with everything we needed to make our way in the world. Now it's time to rest on your laurels. On your fiftieth wedding anniversary, we wish you continued good health and good fortune—and many more years to enjoy them. To Mom and Dad, with love and eternal gratitude!"

Family Toasts

Family members often have occasion to toast one another—birthdays, anniversaries, the receipt of awards or medals, or successes of any other sort.

Child to mother

➢ "We all love our moms, but I defy anyone to find a better one than mine. Mother, you've put up with me through thick and thin, and for that you have my lifelong gratitude. Even more, I thank you for just being the wonderful, intelligent, loving person you are. To Ellen Hawthorne, my beloved mother!"

➢ "The hand that rocks the cradle/Is the hand that rocks the world." (William Ross Wallace)

Child to father

➢ "Here's to my loving father. If before I die I can become just half the person he is, I will have achieved a life well lived."

➤ "Blessed indeed is the man who hears many gentle voices call him father." (Lydia M. Child)

Wife to husband

➤ "Lorenzo swept me off my feet twenty years ago, and he's still pretty cute today. More important, he's the same outstanding, caring person he's always been, as his loving wife and children can confirm! Please join me in a toast to my dear husband."

Husband to wife

➤ "Even if we had lived a century ago, my wife would never have been satisfied with the role of 'the little woman.' On top of a successful nursing career, she's always fought the good fight to make the world a better place. And she did it all while being the best wife a man could ever wish for. To Amy!"

Sibling to sibling

➤ "Sally, if there were an award for best big sister, you'd win hands down. Anyone who could have put up with the likes of me deserves a medal. Thanks for a lifetime of love, warmth, fun, and understanding. To Sally!"

➢ "How good and pleasant it is when brothers dwell in unity!" (Psalm 133:1)

Parents to child

➢ "Life changed forever when you came into the world, Scott, and only for the better. We love you, admire you, and couldn't be more proud of you. To our son, Scott!"

Birthday Toasts

Birthday toasts have plenty of room for humor, so long as you're sure your digs about being "over the hill" won't be taken seriously.

➢ "Yes, Roger, you're forty-five, but I have it on good authority that middle age doesn't start till fifty. And ten years from now, I'll make sure to find the expert who's bumped it up another five years. In any case, we all know there's plenty of life left in the old boy yet. To Roger!"

➢ "Another candle on your cake?/Well, that's no cause to pout./Be glad that you have strength enough/To blow the darn things out." (partydirectory.com)

Holiday Toasts

During the winter holidays, you'll more than likely be taking part in a toast even if no alcohol is consumed.

Christmas

➤ "With all the presents opened and the table cleared, let's remind ourselves of what we're celebrating: the birth of the man who shone a light on the world that will never be extinguished. Please join me in toasting the real spirit of Christmas."

➤ "Here's to all of us . . . God bless us everyone!" (Tiny Tim, in Charles Dickens's *A Christmas Carol*)

New Year's Eve or Day

➤ "Be at war with your vices/At peace with your neighbors/And let every new year find you a new man [woman]." (Benjamin Franklin)

➤ "May you have warm words on a cold evening/A full moon on a dark night/ And the road downhill all the way to your door." (Irish toast)

St. Patrick's Day

➤ "May leprechauns be near you to spread luck along your way/And Irish angels smile upon you on this St. Patrick's Day." (Irish toast)

Fourth of July, Memorial Day, Veteran's Day

➤ "To the wisdom of our Founding Fathers and to every last serviceman and servicewoman who upheld and defended their legacy: freedom for one and all. God bless America!"

Thanksgiving

➤ "May it be God's will that our blessings continue to crowd out our misfortunes and rewards exceed our losses." (Anonymous)

➤ "As we express our gratitude, we must never forget that the highest appreciation is not to utter words, but to live by them." (John F. Kennedy)

Business Toasts

In the business world, the most common times to toast are parties thrown for someone's retirement or the sealing of a business deal and at corporate events that call for full banquets, some of which may be formal enough to require a toastmaster.

To your boss

➤ "Nobody can accuse me of being a kiss-up for what I'm about to say about Ben, because everybody knows it's true. Ben, we appreciate that you have strong opinions but that you still ask for ours. We appreciate your ethics in a time when many bosses are giving big business a bad name. And we wholeheartedly admire your unparalleled managerial skills. Everyone, please join me in toasting a boss we're all blessed to have."

To a retiring employee or a member of the firm

➤ "It's often said that nobody is indispensable, and that may sometimes be the case. But I speak for all of us at Smith and Robbins when I say that there will never be anyone who can replace Jim. Although we'll miss him greatly, we know how much he's looking forward to his retirement—or should I say, 'to life on the golf course'? Jim, we wish you all the happiness you so richly deserve in the years to come."

To a guest of honor at a banquet

➤ "We're gathered here tonight to honor a man who has given unselfishly of his time and effort to make this fundraising campaign so successful.

Without the enthusiasm and leadership that Bob Wells has shown all through these past months, we could never have reached our goal. Please join me in drinking a toast to the man who more than anyone else is responsible for making it possible to see our dream of a new hospital wing finally come true."

➢ "Ladies and gentlemen, you've already heard of the magnificent work our guest of honor has accomplished during her past two years in Washington. Right now we would like to tell her that no matter how proud we are of her success in her chosen career, we're even more pleased to have her home with us again. It's great to have you back, Sharon!"

Toasts for Awards and Accomplishments

Special achievements in sports, academics, or any other field deserve to be acknowledged by toasts from friends, family members, and coworkers.

For a trophy or medal

➢ "We all know the medal Kevin won for the two-hundred-meter butterfly resulted from more than just his ability as a swimmer. It was a testament to his great discipline and resolve, and for that we congratulate him."

For special achievement

➤ "Henry, your fellowship to study overseas will not only expand your horizons but should be your springboard toward achieving even more. We always knew you had it in you, and we wish you a productive and exciting year."

Graduation Toasts

Graduating from high school or college may be one of life's landmarks, but toasts can range from the inspiring to the humorous:

➤ "Here's to Jennifer—whom I've always thought was in a class by herself!"

➤ "Twenty years from now you will be more disappointed by the things you didn't do than by the ones you did do. So throw off the bowlines. Sail away from the harbor. Catch the tradewind in your sails. Explore. Dream. Discover." (Mark Twain)

➤ "Learning is a treasure that will follow its owner everywhere." (Chinese proverb)

Housewarming Toasts

Housewarmings would seem incomplete without the guests expressing their wishes for the hosts' happiness in their new home.

Guests to hosts

➢ "Here's to Dan and Brittany, whose beautiful new house is sure to be filled with warmth, laughter, and love."

Hosts to guests

➢ "May our house always be too small for all of our friends." (Irish toast)

Bon Voyage Toasts

Friends who are about to set off on an extended vacation can be toasted over a dinner with friends or any time a toast seems appropriate.

➢ "May the weather be perfect, the exchange rate in your favor, and the places you visit enrich you with memories forevermore."

➢ "Not traveling is like living in the Library of Congress but never taking out more than one or two books." (Marilyn vos Savant)

FOREIGN-LANGUAGE TOASTS

Reasons for toasting in a foreign language may rarely come your way, but you never know when an international toast may come in handy. For example, you might have good friends whose ties to the old country are strong, and you could surprise them with a toast in their native tongue. Or when traveling abroad, you might find yourself at a dinner or reception where you're expected to make a toast. Following is a sampling of international toasts, with their pronunciations shown in informal phonetics; capital letters indicate the syllable(s) to stress.

Language	Toast	Pronunciation
Arabic	*Besalamati*	beh-suh-la-MAH-tee
Chinese*	*Gan bei*	kahn-BAY
Czech	*Na zdraví*	nahz-DRAHV-ee
Dutch	*Proost*	PROHST
Finnish	*Kippis*	KIP-pis
French	*À vôtre santé*	ah votruh sahn-TAY
German	*Prosit*	PROHST, with guttural R
Greek	*Stin ygia sou*	steen ee-YAH soo
Hebrew	*L'chayim* or *mazel tov*	luh-CHI-um, with guttural CH; MATZ-uhl tohf
Hungarian	*Egészségere*	eh-geh-sheh-GEH-ruh

Language	Toast	Pronunciation
Italian	*Salute* or *cin cin*	sah-LOO-tay; chin-CHIN
Japanese	*Banzai* or *kampai*	BAHN-ZYE; KAHM-PYE
Korean	*Chukbae*	shook-BAY
Malaysian	*Slamat minim*	she-lah-maht MEE-noom
Polish	*Na zdrowie*	nahz-DROH-vee-eh
Portuguese	*A sua saúde*	ah suah SOW-deh
Russian	*Na zdrovye*	nahz-doh-ROH-vee-eh
Scandinavian†	*Skål*	SKOAL
Spanish	*Salud*	sah-LOOD
Turkish	*Serefe*	sheh-REH-feh
Thai	*Choc-tee*	chock-DEE

*Cantonese, Mandarin.
†Danish, Swedish, Norwegian.

INDEX

EMILY POST